SUMMONING THE FATES

Also by Z. Budapest

The Holy Book of Women's Mysteries

Grandmother of Time

Grandmother Moon

Goddess in the Office

Goddess in the Bedroom

Gathering the Goddesses (videotape)

SUMMONING THE FATES

*A Woman's Guide
to Destiny*

Z. BUDAPEST

THREE RIVERS PRESS
NEW YORK

Published by Three Rivers Press, a division of Crown Publishers, Inc.,
201 East 50th Street, New York, New York 10022.
Member of the Crown Publishing Group.

Originally published in hardcover by Harmony Books, a division of
Crown Publishers, Inc., in 1998.

Random House, Inc. New York, Toronto, London, Sydney, Auckland
www.randomhouse.com

Three Rivers Press is a registered trademark of Random House, Inc.

Printed in the United States of America

Design by Barbara Balch

Library of Congress Cataloging-in-Publication Data
Budapest, Zsuzsanna Emese, 1940–
      Summoning the fates : a woman's guide to destiny /
   Z. Budapest.
      (alk. paper)
      1. Women—Religious life.   2. Fates (Mythology).
   3. Fate and fatalism—Miscellanea.   4. Budapest,
   Zsuzsanna Emese, 1940–   .   5. Feminist spirituality.
   6. Goddess religion.   I. Title.
   BL625.7.B84   1998
   305.42—dc21   97-44344

ISBN 0-609-80277-1

First Paperback Edition

This is dedicated to the mystery of the Fates
and the generous unfolding of the Age of Aquarius

ACKNOWLEDGMENTS

Gratitude and deep appreciation to the Fates for the opportunity to summon them back into our times.

Three goddesses helped me to bring this book to fruition. The first one was my agent, Candice Fuhrman, who acted as the fate goddess Urdh by opening the door to new opportunities. I had never had an agent before, so this was certainly an incentive to create a new and worthy book concept. But the Fates were not an easy topic to sum up. Diana Paxson, sister priestess, novelist, and *dynamite* nonfiction writer, manifested the Fate goddess Verdandi by becoming my cowriter and conceptualizer. Diana's contribution to the work has been rich. She shared her own stories, even some of her spells and rituals, and when I got weary, she channeled inspiration. Finally it was the youngest, Laura Wood, my editor, who manifested Skuld because she wielded the final editorial shears. She applied her laser-beam mind and helped to cut away the material that was causing imbalance.

A special thanks to the Latvian National Archives for the safekeeping of so much women's folk poetry, the *dainas* registered there for hundreds of years. These are not so much prayers but conversations with the Dearest Goddess Laima, who is believed to be the sun. And deep thanks to Eso Benjamins, who loved the Dearest Goddess and translated these poems from the original. When I talked with him in the eighties, he told me how much he wished the

Dearest Goddess to be known in the world. I have taken it upon myself to honor some of his translations in this work.

Many artists tried to depict the Fates for the text. How do you capture forces that move all of nature? Finally it was Agusta Agustsson, an artist from Iceland, who gave us these awesome images. In her culture the Fates are still worshiped as of old.

The Fates could not have been understood without the astrologists who have enlightened me about the wheels of life. Thank you to Wendy Ashley for ideas on the ages of the Earth, and for the book she gave me, *Sacred Space* by Geraldine Hatch Hanon. Thank you to Sheila Belanger for the astrological perspective on women's midlife cycle and information on the Skuld years, and also to Martha Betz and Margaret Cole, astrologists, for conversations and notes.

There were many conversations and phone calls, interviews and research that enriched this book. Thanks to the late and terribly missed Jessica Mitford, who encouraged me when I thought my proposal would never be written, and agent Jodi Rein, who stimulated my mind via one single phone conversation to gel many ideas that had been brewing.

Sacred work is a blessing, but friends make up one's life. Marcy Paolocci, a true and longtime best friend, brightened my life and helped when the computer stymied me. And thanks to my little dog, Zoro, who has inspired my next book idea, *Rasta Dog*.

Blessed be!

Contents

Preface

I was always attracted to the idea of the Fates and destiny in general. I wished to get a little bit of a grip on the old questions: Why are we here? What are we doing? What is our mission? I wanted to shout, Is there a script, please? The Fates have one but are not giving it out ahead of time—they unfold it instead. That's okay, just nerve-racking.

So I tried to compose a book where the turning points are listed with their gleaned missions, in order to orient ourselves. Often there is no reason for alarm. A lot of our lives are wasted worrying about something that is on its way.

I used the Latvian *dainas* (poems) to continue this common-sense approach to the Fates. These *dainas* are by women who wrote to their Dearest Goddess as a partner in conversation about love, fate, and all of life.

This book is also an examination of my life and those of my friends and people I admire for these clues. The dance of the fate dates unfolded, as it should. I wrote down and synthesized everything that I know. I am quite certain it's not the whole picture.

The mystery remains.

August 1997
Full Moon

HOW I MET
THE FATES

My mother, Masika Szilagyi, understood all about destiny.

I remember how she stood in front of her green-tile kemence (a tall oven heater for the home) as the men from the museum, dressed in white, carefully carried out her art pieces one by one. There went the statue of the Queen of Heaven, about six feet tall, on a rolling table, and there went the Source Herself, weighing easily three tons. Masika was having a special art show—a pagan temple, she called it—at the Mücsarnok, the Modern Museum, in Budapest. The year was 1977. The show opened on Halloween.

One by one the goddesses she sculpted from clay disappeared from the living room; the place looked empty and sad without them. I stood by, feeling very proud of her. Usually artists had to be dead at least fifty years before they were allowed to show in the Mücsarnok. She motioned me over and pulled the white cloth away from a smaller statue in her hands.

"Look," she whispered, "this is the Holy of Holies. If they take this, you will never see it again. Here," she said. "You take it home."

I had never heard her use such an expression before. Holy of Holies? She was usually very down to earth and would have mocked that kind of terminology at any other time as being overly sentimental. But this was an important moment.

"Mommy," I said, thinking that this rather heavy clay piece would have to travel on my knees all the way to San Francisco, a nineteen-hour plane ride, "isn't this the very center of your pagan temple?"

"Yes, it is. But they will never miss it because they don't expect it—they don't understand the Fates anymore. The Fates are at the center of all creation. I want you to have it. This way I know the very soul of my work will live with you."

I stared at her. This was without doubt the beginning of a new relationship with my mother. She was passing the baton, handing over a tradition. I let her put the piece into my hands, keeping the cloth in place and hugging it to my breast so that the museum men would not notice as they looked around to see if there was anything else they needed to move.

When they were gone, I uncovered the statue. It was a pure white-clay altar piece, divided into three parts, each showing a woman's figure—a spinner, a weaver, and a woman with shears. One started the thread of life, the other developed it, the third one cut it. They had a serenity to them, a simple matter-of-factness, as if they were saying, "This is the way things work. This is life." Yet they contained an unfathomable mystery.

I was very impressed with this simple monochrome altar. The women had no faces. They were clearly spirits. The one in the middle didn't even have hair, just a circle for a face. The loom in her hands rose the highest; she was the tallest one, not seated on tripods like the other two.

"Why do you call them the Holy of Holies?" I asked.

"Because they are representing the secret of life. They are beyond the Goddess. They are like the soul of the Goddess. They are the three Fates."

"The Fates?"

"Yes. Everything is subject to them. Even the gods and goddesses have their own Fates. Governments have them, historical periods have them. Nobody can escape their Fates. They are what must be."

"So the Fates have no rules to follow? No law?"

"Only one: All things must pass. To fulfill this rule is their job."

"All things must pass," I mused, "the good and the bad, the ugly and the beautiful . . ."

"Yes. They distribute all that must be. They cannot just favor you and give you only good things. They cannot skip a historical age just because it is going to be terrible, with war and suffering. They must turn the wheels and make all things manifest."

Mother stroked the three figures with the rough hands of an artist, as if she still wanted to improve on the piece.

"They stand for life and death and everything in between," she added. "They are the sacred technology of life, death, and rebirth."

We sat in the empty living room in the twilight glow from Gellert Mountain, once called Witches' Mountain.

"Here"—she pointed to the first figure—"we are born. Here we flower, and here we die, only to be reborn again."

"Mom, why is this show white? No other color, just white. Isn't that the color of death?"

She acted like somebody caught in a prank.

"Yes, it is. But it is also pure form. No more colors are necessary. I went beyond colors. See how the form creates the lights and shadows on the piece?"

This was a woman who loved colors. She once had a green period that lasted an entire decade. All the artists tried to discover the secret of her glaze, how to get that particular glowing, vibrant, emerald green that only she knew. Then there was a time when she worked up a deep ruby red—that went on for a few years. Once she even did everything in brown. Now here was this white.

"I think I have finished saying what I came here to say," she whispered then.

This scared me. In my family when people have finished their work in life they usually die soon. I started crying.

She was sixty years old when she presented the show at the Mücsarnok, the Modern Museum. A young sixty years old. But I had a strong feeling of foreboding. I had to ask:

"Mom, are you done with this life? Are you fixing to die?"

"I don't know. I just have nothing more to say."

My mother had bloomed early as an artist. Before the war, before she was twenty-five, she was commissioned to create two statues for the city's major plazas. They still stand. The war itself gave her another direction, when she began teaching returning maimed veterans how to do ceramics. She taught them how to throw a pot on the wheel with one leg, and how to paint with your teeth if you've lost both your arms. She also taught women how to survive by creating wicker articles, baskets, and even furniture. Mother was very talented and blessed with humor and optimism.

I was extremely glad that I had come to see her in her glory. I knew how much she loved the fact that I'd come all the way from California. She showed me off to her friends. Here at home, I was no longer Z. Budapest, but "Masika's daughter."

"Mom, when you do die, should I come home to your funeral?" I asked suddenly. I needed to clear this up if she was really thinking of dying. Budapest is so far away from California.

I had never heard my mother talk about her death, mostly because she was so deeply engaged with life. But because I was holding the Fates in my lap, death seemed to be a proper line of conversation.

She smiled a little and stroked my face, smearing the tears on my cheeks.

"I don't know, *kislanyom*"—my little girl—"but I certainly won't be there."

"You won't be there? At your funeral?" I started laughing, relieved that we were getting back into our normal stride, back to the joking, the lighthearted banter.

"No, only my body will be. A funeral is more for the living than the dead. I'll be with Grandma. And right after I see her, I want to visit Rodin."

She was already making plans.

"And when you come back, will I know you again?" I probed.

"Maybe. Maybe not. I may not come back very soon. It's best to let go."

Grief overwhelmed me again. I cried with the wrenching sobs of a child being separated from her mother. She got up and took the statue back from me and stood it upright on the table against the white wall. The whiteness of everything just intensified my feeling that I was losing her.

"You found me this lifetime; it can happen again," she said to console me.

That was the last time I saw my mother. She died three years later while writing a letter to me. Her handwriting trailed off as she dropped the pen. I still have that letter, of course, in my own Holy of Holies, a little collection of family relics, a strand of Grandmother's hair, and a little pinch of Hungarian soil that I took with me when I escaped from the Russians.

I didn't go to her funeral. For me she is still alive. For the funeral, my brother Imre burned frankincense and myrrh, and hired a gypsy band to sing her folk songs to put her to sleep. Hundreds of people who loved her art came to see her off. She was in the lap of the Fates. Back in the original cauldron. She was one with the Source.

Memories flood my mind when I think about the studio where my mother sculpted, cooked dinner for her students and me, painted, and told her stories. The place was full of statues—small ones, tall ones, big ones. Most of her imagery was mythological. There was Boldog-Asszony, goddess of fruits and harvest, who was seven feet tall. And there was the goddess as Source, who was six feet tall, a round, intricate creation with wheels within wheels, turning and churning. You had to walk around the piece to get the full impact. On her right and left shoulders were the faces of Adam and Eve, still part of the same mother, not yet differentiated. Later she made them separately out of terra-cotta, a flesh-colored clay, the only pieces that were not white in her show. The sexes were separate now, projected out of the Source. Adam and Eve looked lonely. My mother also made many different folk Madonnas for home altars. The Hungarian peasants loved to buy their home altars from her, but her Madonnas were always holding a girl baby, not a little Jesus. Nobody cared.

Out of all the rich heritage she left to us, the statue she gave me was the only one in which my mother portrayed the Parcae, the three Fates. She had the utmost reverence for them. She prayed to them, offered toasts to them, and poured out a little of her wine on the ground to them. But she sculpted them only this one time. The altar piece hangs in my bedroom today—the first thing I see when I wake up and the last thing when I go to sleep. It's my permanent prayer.

Somehow, in this statue, my mother's voice is still present. When I have big questions I can always pause under it and ask them. Maybe not right away, but soon enough I will have my answer. Whether it is my own inner voice that speaks to me, or somebody says something out of the blue that has a direct relationship to what I'm wondering about, the answer comes.

For a year and a half I was searching for the theme of my new book. Was it going to be about the winds of change? The different revolutions I have witnessed? Was it going to be about my life: "Zsuzsanna the Hun"? Was it going to be another book on life's passages? I stood under the little statue of the Fates and angrily demanded an answer. This time I heard the voices.

"Investigate us. We are alive."

What? I had to sit down. The obvious is always the hardest to hear.

"Call upon us. We are still here."

I closed my eyes—cutting off outer vision makes it easier to see inner truth—and took a few deep breaths to center my soul. It seemed to me that suddenly the air was cool and fresh, the way it is near a stream. In fact I could hear the bubbling of water somewhere nearby, and the whisper of wind in leaves.

"Who are you today? What do we call you?" I asked.

"Destiny. Forever and always we are destiny," came the ghostly answer.

In my mind's eye the shadows were lifting. I saw the great trunk of a tree whose roots arched overhead so that I seemed to be in a cavern. The sound of water came from a great well. Somehow the three figures in the statue had been transported to the cavern. They were sitting, spinning out thread, and staring at me expectantly.

"I can't write about you," I objected. "Where are your temples, where are the inscriptions?"

"In your soul, the Goddess is returning," said one.

"The millennium is turning," said the second.

"A new cycle is beginning," said the third.

"We are where we always were—in the old stories you tell your children, in the movements of the stars, in your hearts."

I thought about it.

"You mortals are always talking about us, but you just don't use the right names," said one. "You always want to know what is going to happen, so you talk to psychics, channelers, mediums, witches. You read cards; you check out the astrology column in the newspaper. Look around you; listen to the expressions you use. You're talking to us all the time!"

"Did you buy a lottery ticket this week?" asked another. "When you gamble, you are trying to get our attention, daring us to touch and bless you."

"We never went away," said the third. "We are younger than anybody and older than the hills. We are your contemporaries. Listen to us, and we'll tell you what to write. We're tired of being ignored!"

"Yes, ma'am," I said. Then the phone rang and the vision vanished. But when the Fates talk to you that clearly, you don't say no.

So here I am, passing down the tradition of the Fates to a new generation. I am gathering together their lost "stuff": their properties and characteristics that were stolen or assimilated by other gods; their holy names; their colors and customs; their mythology. The Fates' wisdom has been dispersed all over the globe, hidden in language and embroidery, folk dances and sayings, sacred rites and superstitions. But most of all, their challenges are hidden in our aging process. No matter what our age, we are living out their natural laws. To know the Fates is to be more comfortable in life's flow. To keep studying the Fates is to accumulate wisdom for our peace of mind. The Fates are medicine for the soul.

May they never again be forgotten.

CIRCLES WITHIN CIRCLES

I don't make
my song;
I only sing it.
I sing my song
with words
given to me by
the Dearest Goddess.

LATVIAN WOMEN'S FOLK POEM
NO. 35802.224

On the freeway near my house there's a billboard advertising the lottery, with a picture of a bag of money and the words "You could be next!"

The other day I complimented a friend on her hair. "Thank you," she said, "but I can't take any credit for it. Curly hair runs in my family."

A friend of mine was in a car accident, then he lost his job, and then his cat ran away. "What did I do to deserve this?" he asked. "Am I doomed to be a failure?"

I know two women, best friends through college. One got married right after graduation to a successful man and had a son and a daughter. The other got a job with an accounting firm and began to fight her way up the corporate ladder toward a vice-presidency. They were sure they had found their destinies. But by the time they had reached thirty, the one who was married had left her husband and started law school, and the accountant had quit her job to start a flower shop.

It makes you wonder.

What rules our lives? Is it chance, or choice, or something else? Is it the stars, or that strange force people call Lady Luck, or Fortuna? Since the beginning of time, people have tried to figure out what determines their destiny. In Hungary we have a saying, *"Ember tervez, Isten vegez"*—"Humans plan, God finishes."

But the Fates are beyond even goddesses and gods. They are raw forces of nature. They are rhythms of the ebb and flow of energy, matter, and meaning—the three basic components of the universe. They were here first; they will stay to the last. Everyone's story is in the Fates' web. They are one; they are three; they are nine, three times three. Their mystery cannot be totally understood, or can it? All the other goddesses and gods became their emanations through time.

It was the fate of Zeus to destroy his own father. The Norse gods cannot avoid Ragnarok. When the gods must obey the Fates, you know who is in charge.

This archetype of destiny is embedded deep in the Indo-European psyche. From India across the European continent all the way to the North Sea and the British Isles, cultures big and small have stories, symbols, and ceremonies for the forces who make destiny. Some of these overlap, some diverge, but they agree on the fundamental concept. There are three sisters who rule our lives.

The three Weird sisters are working women. They are spinners, weavers, cutters of the thread; they are writers of the Book of Life. They are blessers, birthers, deathers, dressed in white and red and black. They are fortune-tellers. They are casters of the lots. They are gamblers and luck-givers. They are living springs of water. They are mornings, noons, and nights. What they rule must be.

Since the dawn of consciousness people have found it psychologically useful to give names and faces to the Fates. The Greeks called them the *Parcae;* the Romans, *Fata;* in northern Europe they were the *Norns,* who governed men's "wyrd," or fate, and for Anglo-Saxons, the "weird" were those who could foretell the future.

I am especially fond of the word *wyrd,* because we use it today when something happens that we don't understand, cannot control, or fear. The word comes from a form of the old Germanic verb meaning "to become."When we feel something is weird, we activate our fate receptors, the soul that knows the Fates intimately already. Only the soul can understand something weird—the action itself, the presence of the Fates, and their effect on our lives. Often we resist their promptings, only to appreciate them later on.

I had to grow up and discover the Fates for myself. The discovery, however, did not come from a book; rather, it was a living process. I had to become aware. You don't really understand what the Fates can do to you unless you have had a visceral experience of them.

During the Hungarian revolution in October of 1956, I was on my way to a demonstration. When you are sixteen, being part of a collective uprising is very exciting. I lived on the Buda side of the Duna River, and to reach the site of the demonstration, I had to cross the bridge over to the Pest side. I was running toward the bridge when suddenly something weird happened. My feet slowed as if they were weighted down with lead. Frustrated, I redoubled my efforts, but try as I might, I could only shuffle along, furious that I was going to be late.

When I finally crossed the bridge, I heard shots. That wasn't too unusual. It was a revolution, and people had been shooting off guns in celebration for days. But when I turned the corner to the plaza, everything was silent. Too silent. Instead of a crowd of cheering, shouting people, the plaza was covered with bodies. All those who had made it to the plaza on time had been shot down. The blood was still dripping onto the stones. I stood stock-still, realizing that I had indeed arrived too late—too late for the massacre.

In Hungarian the Fates are *Sors Istennök,* the destiny goddesses. But their Latin name, the *Parcae,* means "those who spare," and indeed my life was spared by them that day. We all have stories about incidents during which that weird feeling, usually accompanied by fear or frustration, has come over us, and it turned out to save us in some way.

The English name for the Fates comes from the Latin word *fata*. In the singular, the word was *fatum,* meaning "a divine utterance," the will of a god. When a child was a week old, the *fata scribundus* were invoked to "write" a good destiny for the newborn babe. The *fata,* with the birth goddess Eileithyia, both established and predicted the child's destiny. The word *fate, fatum,* comes from the same root as the words *fairy* and *fay.* So we learn the Fates are of fairy origin.

In Greek they were called the *Moirae,* those who allot us our fate; there was Clotho (the Spinner), who spins the thread of life, Lachesis (Disposer of Lots), who measures it out, and Atropos (the Inevitable), who cuts it off. Clotho is usually portrayed with a spindle, Lachesis with a scroll or a globe, and Atropos with scissors, a pair of scales, or a bowl for drawing lots.

When they are in good spirits, these same Fates become the three Graces. You may have seen them represented in Botticelli's *Primavera* or the Three Graces statue at the Getty Museum in Malibu. They are three lush women entwined in dance with one another. Their names are Aglaia (Radiant), Euphrosyne (Joy), and Thalia (Flowering). They are the companions of Aphrodite. When the Fates are angered, they are called the Furies; they pursue you like ill winds blowing and can punish with insanity. Then their names are Alecto, Tisiphone, and Magaera. They cannot be avoided. It is said that the Fates are the parthenogenetic daughters of Necessity. They have no father. They sit under the Tree of Life next to the sacred spring, where they spin and prophesy, make pronouncements, and enforce natural law.

In northern Europe we also find three maidens who sit beside a well in a deep cavern. These are the Norns, from the Germanic traditions, best known today from their appearance in Wagner's opera *Götterdämmerung.* They are named in Old Norse: Urdh, Verdandi, and Skuld. Their names come from the words for *being itself,* and so I will use these names for the Fates in this book.

Urdh (the same word as *wyrd* and *weird*) is all that went before. She is the past. She owns the Well of Life and the Tree of Life, which is fed by the well. Everything that has ever been belongs to the past. From this fertile background life emerges anew.

Verdandi, whose name means "that which is becoming," rules what is going on right now. She is flux. She is the flower of our energies. She is the mother time, the ripe time, the sexual time. She is harvest time. Her symbol is the full loom.

Skuld (whose name is related to "shall") is the one who governs that which must be. She is the necessary outcome of the past and that which is becoming. Skuld is the inflexible one, but in some later legends, she likes to ride with humans and mingle with men. She is the one who may request a kiss from a handsome man and change into a beautiful young woman if he has enough gumption to kiss her old face. Strangely, the most personable of the Fates turns out to be the death goddess. Her symbol is the crescent knife, the ghostly scythe of the Grim Reaper. The Grim Reaper is a girl.

This original model of the three sisters is the source for all the other triple goddesses, such as Hecate, who stands at the triple crossroads, her faces looking in three directions—the past, present, and future—and Triple Brigid, who appears as a healer, a goldsmith, and a lady of inspiration. It is the pattern for the trinities of maiden, mother, and crone and all the other goddesses who have three aspects. Each of the many components of our human existence required the Goddess to show a separate face and attributes. Eventually the original trinity became ten thousand aspects, each with her own name, each still harking back to the beginning, the middle, or the end of the life cycle, which the three Fates rule.

When we summon the Fates, we call them out from their deep hiding place in the unconscious. We draw them slowly into the conscious mind, illuminated by goodwill and understanding.

This eternal magic can transform the powers that rule us from the misunderstood three Hags into the wonderful three Graces. Or at least we hope so. There are no guarantees with this force. But there are certain practices, a kind of etiquette of interaction with the Fates, that have worked for people before. We call it the technology of the sacred.

"Sacred" means that we are speaking not of a technology of machines but of souls. We behave differently and do unusual things to relate to an unseen divine force. Prayer, for example, is such a sacred technology. Creating sacred space is another. Traveling between the worlds in meditation is one as well, and blessings and cursings are others.

As they learned about the likes and dislikes of the Fates, people created ways to talk to them. When you mention their names, you should always show a great deal of respect. The Fates live in each DNA cell in our bodies. This is why they can hear everything everywhere. We invoke them in our language. "Good morning," for example, a blessing to set the tone for the day, evokes the name of Morgana la Fay, a Celtic fate goddess. We say "good night" to ward off bad dreams. Some say language was created in order to call to the Fates. Small acts of living reveal their familiar powers—holy water sprinkled around in a room to purify it against bad luck, and clinking glasses before making a toast in an effort to have your blessings heard by the Fates so they can fulfill them.

Weddings have many kinds of good-luck rituals. As protection against the evil eye, the groom is not supposed to look at the bride before the wedding (the same reason that the bride's head is protected with a veil). Where does the custom of wearing something old, something new, something borrowed, and something blue, come from? It's a charm to honor the Fates, who are both old and new, who are a connection to the community (borrowed), whose favorite color is blue. At Jewish weddings the guests call out *"mazel tov"*—"good luck"—as the groom breaks the glass in the white napkin. The jumping of the broom in pagan weddings signifies the couple's wish to stay together, as they leap hand in hand into the future; the broom itself is a piece of the Tree of Life and, as such, is used to invoke good luck for the couple.

The colors of the Fates are red, black, and white. In Transylvania there are Hungarian tribes famous for the beauty of their embroidery. When weaving started as a sacred activity, bestowing protection and blessings with each stitch, there were laws governing how many colors an embroiderer could use; and to this day they use these three colors only. Red is for life's blood; black is for life, because it includes all colors; and white is for death, or the spirit, because it is drained of all color. These Fate colors are repeated on wall hangings, bed covers, tablecloths to bring good luck into the home. In other regions household linens are embroidered with pictures of doves, roses, and blue forget-me-nots. The embroidery on wedding coats and jackets for work all contain images of the good luck invoked, the protection requested. Decorations on our clothes started as a prayer to the Fates. Our ancestors had lucky jackets, lucky boots, lucky shirts, lucky necklaces, and, of course, blankets for dreaming. Any kind of good-luck charm is a symbol of the Fates. A horseshoe pointed downward, for example, stands for the opened cornucopia from which good luck comes.

Experience taught me that you could summon the Fates whenever the need arose, in a crisis or at a great celebration. The Fates could hear things carelessly uttered, such as a boast, or the words that slip out unconsciously in moments of great fear, joy, or even ecstasy. Dying was another fateful time, when it was believed that words uttered with the last breath could come true. Words were powerful, especially the ones you said without thinking. For example, it was thought that if you bragged about your good fortune, your luck would soon turn. There were all kinds of rituals to protect your good luck. Universally, the favorite one was to knock on wood three times. Why on wood and not bronze or iron? Because the Fates belong to the Tree of Life, and all wood is considered to come from that sacred tree.

Everyone understood that luck had to be balanced. The Greeks honored this idea in the form of the goddess Nemesis, who punished those who upset the natural balance and proportion, whether because of excessive good fortune or, more often, by the arrogance it often brings. Her emblems were the measuring rod, bridle, and yoke, which were used to exert control, and the sword and scourge with which to punish the proud. Such is a law of nature. Today we encounter it most often in the environment, where suppressing one problem can often cause a worse one. In California, for instance, wildfires are a natural part of the ecology: When you prevent them for too long, underbrush builds up, and a single spark can set off an inferno.

In Hungary, if you wanted to praise a baby, you said the opposite. It was very important to protect it from the evil eye by saying something like "Wow, that baby is not half bad!" or even to lie, saying, for example, "What an ugly baby!" The young mother then would certainly know that you loved her baby. If happiness finally got hold of you, and you felt like shouting it to the universe, my mother always added, "Praise be the Fates!" and cautioned with her eyes not to overdo it, lest the happiness be short-lived.

The etiquette for observing nature's special favors alone could fill a book. In Hungary if a bird deposits its poopoo on your head while you are waiting for a bus or walking about, it is considered very good luck. Wiping it away would erase the blessing. Stepping into dog doodoo also means good luck, but in this case you are allowed to wipe it clean, thank heaven.

So who are these crotchety ladies who are listening in every room, hiding in every tree? And why is poopoo sacred to them? Why is that good luck? Because they are the compost and the seed; they are the flower and the fruit; they are the green tree and the rotting grave.

The Fates are the conductors of luck. They preside over uncertainty. They do not play favorites, even if it sometimes seems to us that they are doing so. This is why we accept the "luck of the draw." They are nonpolitical and are beyond all religions. They are the forces that are. They are life.

CYCLES WITHIN CYCLES

We talk about the past, present, and future as if the Fates operated in a straight line, but at each point in our lives we must deal with the effects of what has already happened, cope with what we are facing now, and prepare for what is to come. We are never done with the past, because it is always being created by what we are doing now, and that, in turn, becomes the future. We interact with Urdh, Verdandi, and Skuld in a sacred spiral cycle in which the same lessons are repeated, although in different ways, again and again.

Throughout your childhood, for instance, certain cycles were repeated. Every time you started a new level of school, you progressed from the equivalent of freshman to graduate. Now, whenever you start a new job, you move through a period of probation and gradually attain seniority. There are cycles in relationships as well—the exciting, uncertain weeks in which you are getting to know each other, wondering how the other person really feels; the comfortable stage when you are at ease with each other; and then, if you are lucky, a time of deepening that goes below surface interactions until you understand each other's souls. But fate is not fixed. Sometimes you don't graduate, you never do become a senior, and all relationships can sour.

Each year is a cycle, when the sleep of winter gives way to the awakening of spring, summer's fruitfulness, autumn's harvest, and finally the cold sleep of winter again. The longer cycles of drought or rainfall often take us by surprise, but a long-term study of climate shows that they, too, are a part of the natural spiral.

Many cultures, from Hindu to Mayan, view the history of the earth not as a pair of lines pointing backward and forward from the year 1 A.D., but rather as a series of ages, each of which comes into being, reaches maturity, and concludes. We speak of decades, such as "the sixties," as separate time periods, each of which develops, matures, and fades. Just now, we are in the final years not only of a century, but of a millennium, and though reason tells us that January 1, 2000, will not be much different from January 1, 1999, psychologically it is another story. Already stories about people who fear that the end of the millennium will be the end of the world are beginning to hit the airwaves.

The Fates do not act at random, except at that first fateful moment when the Spinner pulled us out of her cauldron of infinite possibilities. Once we are drawn into existence, however, natural law takes over. At certain points in our lives we face decisions and changes. These "fate dates" are times at which it is especially productive to consciously work with destiny. Some of these times are biological, such as puberty and menopause. Others can be charted by looking at the stars. In particular, the "Saturn return" cycle, in which Saturn moves around the zodiac to return to the point in the sky where it was located when you were born, has a powerful effect on destiny.

The first Saturn cycle, from birth to age twenty-eight and three-quarters, is under the guardianship of Urdh, who rules the past. In this first cycle of our lives, we learn the potential and limitations of the bodies that our genes and our environment have given us, and work out the psychological implications of our family and cultural heritage. Whether we are fulfilling parental expectations or rebelling against them, we are responding to the past.

In the second Saturn cycle, ruled by Verdandi, we "become" ourselves. By now most of us have worked through our old hang-ups, and Verdandi gives us a new mission. We know now who we are and what we can do. We settle into careers and relationships, build families, discover our missions in life.

The third cycle, beginning around age fifty-six or so, opens the door to yet another destiny. This is the realm of Skuld—what shall be. Gradually we break loose from the bonds that we forged for ourselves in Verdandi and give birth to a new self that has been slowly maturing within. We have done everything our parents thought we should do, as well as the things that we thought we should do. We even perform stunning reversals. In Skuld's cycle, the soul can fly free.

Our own astrological cycles interact with the larger cycles that determine the ages of the earth, both the long zodiacal ages and the sub-ages into which they are divided. For instance, although the true "Age of Aquarius" will not begin until the twenty-fourth century, we are now in an Aquarian sub-age that started in 1962, has colored the subsequent decades, and will last until the year 2141. This sub-age of Aquarius previews in many ways what the *actual* age will be like.

As we go through life, experience teaches us how to deal with change. But we will work with our Fates much more effectively when we learn to recognize the turnings of the wheel. At each point, half of a "chance" is ours to make. The Fates hold the other half.

FATEGRAPH

No matter which generation you are traveling with, there are certain points at which the Fates touch you more than at others, visit you more often, change you more deeply. Even the Fates have their times and seasons. We sense this in portents of things to come. These fate dates are based on astrology, which tells us when the relationships of the planets to those in our birth chart indicate turning points in our lives. These are not just the obvious connections we see reported in the Sunday papers, such as the day of birth (although obviously birthdays are major celebrations of our existence); but other, less-recognized portentous times are equally important.

Without turning you into an astrologer, let's just start by saying that the dance of the Fates is complex, with smaller cycles nestled within larger ones. Even if you know everything there is to know about certain fate dates and their purpose, the mystery of life will still not be explained.

The big wheels of life form the procession of the great ages. Within that cycle we have the sub-ages that determine our particular time period's flavor. Within each sub-age the three transpersonal planets, Neptune, Pluto, and Uranus, influence the social/psychic orientation of the generations as their cycles move through the signs of the zodiac.

Now hold on. Within the span of the generational patterns into which we are born, we experience the personal planets' shaping force. These personal planets are the Moon, the Sun, Mercury, Venus, and Mars. Their cycles moving through the zodiac sculpt our character. Are you still dancing?

The maturing, changing self needs one more combination, another wheel of time, to turn our passages. It is the mother lode planet Saturn, whose slow movement turns the three major destiny points of our lives. Finally, we need Uranus to administer a cosmic shift that often is experienced as a fated accident from which new developments can spring.

As you will see throughout this book, within the major turning points of the Saturn returns there are times when the other planets, such as Neptune, Uranus, and Pluto, influence us with their energies. On these fate dates you can see how certain issues come to the fore in your life and need to be addressed for your soul's progress. Being able to look back on the fate dates of your life will help you see the unfolding of the larger pattern of the story of your life. Being able to anticipate upcoming fate dates will allow you to consciously engage with their energies and do your part by fulfilling your potential and using your free will. You will find it pleasurable to gain this skill for conscious living.

I have included the following fategraph to show your fate dates and the soul's skill associated with each date.

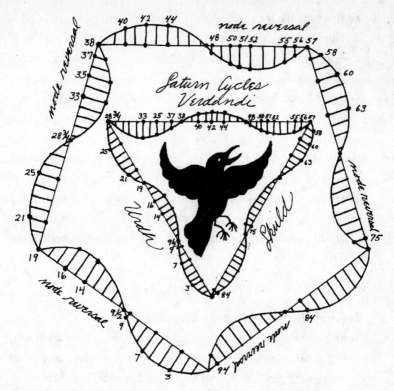

The Nodes of the Norns—Creativity / Fertility Cycles

DATES WHEN THE FATES ARE VERY PRESENT

These are the auspicious times that you could use to commemorate with rituals and celebrations.

Urdh's Dance

First destiny: Get a life.

Birth: Purifications for the renewal of the mother and the blessing of the child.

Day 7: The first moon-quarter of life. Naming rituals and receiving the new baby into the community.

Year 3: A quarter of the Jupiter cycle. Blessings on the child. The soul reveals its purpose, so watch your child carefully. Ask your child questions of a cosmic nature. They are sages at this age.

Years 7 to 9: Initiation into the spirit world and acknowledging the spiritual nature of the child. New sacred name given for the spirit. Begin to do rituals.

Year 14: First half of Saturn cycle. Time to go to work on some project of great interest. Initiation into womanhood.

Year 21: Initiation of the first Fate, Urdh. Three-quarters through the Saturn cycle, serving the first Fate. Assumption of full personal responsibility. Playing out the scenario of the first destiny.

Verdandi's Dance

Second destiny: Bloom, get another life.

Year 28¾: First full Saturn return. Completion of the adult self. Initiation into the second destiny. Remember the many other energy curves that end up here. Fundamental life changes.

Years 33 to 34: Questioning authority seriously. You have lots of turmoil in your life now, but hang in there and endure. Look out for a new mission to be revealed—it's in your face!

Years 37 to 38: Saturn squares Saturn. Your soulwork is to dismantle all false identities. Be honest with yourself. Build up the dream.

Years 37 to 48: Pluto squares Pluto. Your soulwork is to confront powerlessness and victimhood. Integrate your shadows and the parts of yourself you have denied so far.

Years 38 to 42: Uranus opposite Uranus. Midlife transition and sudden changes. Watch for reversals! Go with them and don't be afraid.

Years 41 to 42: Mystical awakening. Your soulwork is creativity, spell work, ritual work, writing about the soul, and mellowing out. Loving. Review your past from a spiritual point of view. Reflect.

Years 43 to 44: Your soulwork is to resolve all childhood or youthful hurts. Healing of the old self (inner child). Forgiving. In ancient Rome the Vestal virgins were released from temple duty to reenter normal life at this time. Vows taken earlier in life are now fullfilled.

Years 51 to 52: The comet Chiron returns. The wounded healer is taking us to a different reality. Your soulwork is to confront mortality, which is not easy. You could sustain a new wounding, so brace yourself and be careful.

Years 56 to 58: Second Saturn return—Verdandi's destiny ends and Skuld greets you. All the other curves converge in this time of our lives. It's as momentous as the first Saturn return, but you are more prepared for it. Wisdom is coming! Peace of mind is coming, too, but if you have neglected the soul until now, you may have to play catch-up.

Skuld's Dance

Third destiny: Simplify. Express yourself.

Years 60 to 62: Uranus squares Uranus. This is the time to review your leftover rebellions and give some of them inner action. Submerge in the holiness of the everyday or pursue relentlessly a key action for liberation.

Year 63: Cronehood really begins to take shape. Your new self-identity is emerging. Your priorities are different now. If you were giving your energy to others all your life, you are now taking in energy for yourself. If you were taking in energy from others all your life, now you will have to give some back.

Years 65 to 66: Saturn squares Saturn. Deeper stability is needed. Review what it would take to look after yourself better. The structure of your lifestyle should be worked on and stabilized.

Years 71 to 72: The sixth Jupiter return. Time to drop into the energy of wisdom about getting older. There is much joviality and wisdom to share, especially in your family circle.

Years 72 to 73: Saturn opposes Saturn. Be careful of hardships and accidents. This is a dangerous time.

Years 79 to 80: The third-quarter square Saturn. Simplify even more. Review the changes you made at 72 to 73 and try to improve on them. You understand soulwork now. Spirituality is a priority more than ever.

Years 85 to 86: Pluto opposes Pluto. Confront death and learn to see her as another state of intimacy. Prepare to enter the spirit world.

Years 87 to 88: The third Saturn return and the end of Skuld's destiny for you. You are on your own now, kid! How did you surrender control to Skuld? A little at a time. Bless us as you become our ancestor.

URANUS'S STEPS—YOUR MISSION CURVE

From birth to 21 years: You achieve your first personality. Many of us look back on old photographs and see a stranger looking back at us. We sigh, "Oh, that was another lifetime!" Well, it was. This time is the soul's first opus.

Years 21 to 42: This is the age of the great quest. In this time and space you will stumble across your big adult mission, the one that will contribute to the collective consciousness of the world. This quest simply will reveal itself. You cannot "plan" for it. It emerges about age 30 and unfolds by age 42. There is enough time here to have two missions, maybe even opposing ones. It can happen. However, this is the prime time. You have energy for great achievements. Most of life's work is done in this space.

Years 42 to 63: You experience a reorganization of your understanding of your mission. Achievement is still building, but a very different angel may be guiding you, or you may have found a related mission to the already-completed one. If, on the other hand, you haven't had any missions so far, now is the time to jump on the platform. This is often a time for women when the kids are leaving home—and perhaps even the husbands. Doors open and instead of frightening yourself to death or drowning in bitterness, say thank you, and embark on the adventure yet ahead. Energy and luck are with you when you dance the dance of life.

Years 63 to 84: We remove ourselves from the battlefield. Or we enter the battlefield if we have not been on it yet. All things must pass. Look at all the Gray Panthers fighting and changing laws. Our society will see more and more older people taking to the streets in defense of the forest, wildlife, and animal rights. A good example of this is former President Jimmy Carter, who builds houses for the poor in his seventies and recites poetry.

After 84, kick back, for heaven's sake, and write your memoirs!

THE MOON CURVE AND FERTILITY CYCLES

From birth to 19 years: We mature into the first fertile adult self. Menses sets in and you have huge sexual surges. Your hormones are in their youthful peak. Many women get married or pregnant at this time.

Years 19 to 38: You experience your fertility energy, making this a good time to make babies. The desire for marriage and all kinds of bonding is intense now. This is the time to fall in and out of love and have the ecstasy and agony of an intense emotional life. If you live through many turmoils now, you have something to write about later on. Open your heart and feel fully.

Years 38 to 56: Wisdom starts seeping in like rain through a leaky roof. Menopause weans you from your estrogen highs and lows, and you can feel the inner shifts of changing fates. The crone arrives into your body and you enter a new incarnation.

Years 56 to 75: Another full cycle occurs when we transform fertility into wisdom. Foolish people who have never risked or lived fully stay foolish, however. Age is not a guarantee of wisdom, but it is hard to escape gaining some.

Years 75 to 94: Another full cycle occurs. This is a time of life yet to be experienced by the soul-conscious generation. It is a relatively unexplored era of life because our species has not yet lived this long en masse. If we're lucky enough to do so, though, we should return to some form of spirituality.

THE MIND CURVE

It's all up, up, up until the second Saturn return at the ages of 56 to 58. Here you start clueing in to moderation. Sensibilities emerge that you didn't have before. Balance is a form of wisdom.

Year 60: We have a Jupiter return, a joyous expansion of consciousness, when profound realizations are possible.

Year 63: Uranus has achieved three quarters of its cycle. This is an initiation for the journey home. You start thinking about retirement and start contemplating life beyond this one.

Year 74: Your Saturn has arrived once again to its natal point—a Saturn return is always momentous. This is the going-within time. You are happy to tune inward toward your soul. For some people these are hermetic years; for others, soul-work is communal work.

Year 84: We get a Uranus return, the bringer of memories. This is a very good time to remember the past. Write, dictate, reflect.

WORKING: FEAST OF THE FATES

To work with the Fates, you need to connect with them at the deepest level, the level that goes beyond words, the level of ritual. Symbols are the vocabulary of the unconscious, and ritual is its language. The rituals in this book are messages that your mind sends to your soul. Since the Fates operate below the level of conscious awareness, a ceremony such as the following will help you to invite them into your life.

The first step is to clear your mind of fear of the unknown, no small task, since that is where the Fates abide. Then prepare yourself by gathering significant objects, such as a magical pendant, or by centering yourself with a ritual, such as breathing in power, exhaling weakness. Open your home for the Feasts of the Fates; the traditional date is June 24, the eve of the summer solstice (according to the old calendar), but you can give them a feast at any time, such as when you begin to work with this book.

I lay the feast before the little statue of the Fates that my mother made, but you will not find one of those in any store. Instead, you can use a statue or a picture of the three Graces, or you can just use three candles—white, red, and black. If you live near a store that sells votive candles, you may be able to find candles in the shape of goddesses. Set up your altar with a white cloth and the images or candles. If you use a statue, also include the candles in the appropriate colors. You can decorate the altar with flowers as well.

The Fates like red foods and red drinks—they stimulate them—so cook a meal with food that has red in it and share it with friends. Try red beans with sausage, for example, and red sweet peppers. Serve red wine and, for dessert, raspberries and red grapes or berry pie. Set the three ladies their own small plates, treating them as if they were present—because they are. Toast them and talk to them. All you say will be heard, so don't make frivolous jokes. The Weird sisters are not invited often into modern consciousness, let alone to dinner, and they will be impressed.

Thank them eloquently and warmly for the gifts you have received in the past. Ask for their help in recognizing the gifts and opportunities that are coming to you now, and ask them to guide you so that you will be in the right place, and the right frame of mind, to benefit in the future. Close your eyes and sit for a few moments in silence. Concentrate on your breath. Clear your mind by noting all your busy thoughts and gently nudging them away. When the internal monologue slows down, "listen" and note what new thoughts come to you. This is how the Fates speak to those who know how to listen.

When you are finished, thank the Fates for their presence and nip out the candles with your fingers (you can light them again for other workings). Then give the food from their plates to hungry dogs, maybe your own pets. The Fates, like Hecate, love hounds.

As you read this book, remember the "messages" that came to you during the feast. Before you start each new chapter, close your eyes and ask the Fates to open your heart and teach you what you need to know.

Your growing consciousness is the fertile soil of imagination, and imagination transforms into fuel for consciousness. If you let go, your inner voice will come—not on cue, but always on time.

AN APRON FULL OF GOLD

I see you
sowing silver,
Dearest Goddess,
all around
the seashore.
Sow,
Dearest Goddess,
a share
for me.
An acre
or two
will do.

LATVIAN WOMEN'S FOLK POEM
NO. 33661.229

In the old fairy stories, the Fates give luck to some people as a naming present at their first birthday. These people go through life beneath a series of showers of gold, whereas other people get covered with tar and never seem to get free. But is luck fated? Fairy tales tell us a different story.

There are many fairy tales about a maiden who has to serve an old woman and perform difficult tasks without understanding what the test really is until she has passed or failed. The old woman is life itself. She is the seasons and the challenges and the necessary trivia. The lesson she teaches is that one must be faithful in small things in order to win fame and fortune.

What adolescents rarely understand is that the teenage girl remains alive inside the grown woman—even in the old woman who is telling the story. Fairy tales have such enduring popularity because the challenges faced by the protagonists recur again and again in our lives. In the cycle of fate, we are continually being shaped by Urdh, moving into the eternal present of Verdandi, and looking forward to Skuld's future. And so it is never too late to shake out Mother Holle's pillows.

Mother Holle is a familiar figure from German folklore. Once she was worshiped as a goddess, called Holde or Huld or Holle. Traditionally, she is a queenly and beneficent figure who drives about in a wagon, but she can also ride the winds, clothed in terror. Sometimes she appears as a lovely lady bathing in a lake, but more often she has the appearance of "an ugly old woman, long-nosed, big-toothed, with bristling and thick-matted hair" (*Teutonic Mythology,* p. 269). She is called Mother Holle, but it must be remembered that "mother" is a term of respect offered by adults to women of their own mother's age.

Holle's particular interests are household matters. She dislikes disorder and will help an industrious spinster. It was said that all the flax in the house must be spun by New Year's and the spindles put away or she would punish the lazy. She has survived to the present day hidden in this story, which is preserved in *Grimm's Fairy Tales.*

There was once a young girl who lived with her stepmother and stepsister near the forest. Her stepmother was not kind, and since the girl was very good at spinning, her stepmother kept her hard at work. One day she was sitting on the rim of a well, spinning flax (which must be kept damp in order to twine), when she dropped her spindle down the well. Afraid to be punished for losing it, she jumped in after it down the well, but instead of splashing into dark water, she found herself in a lovely meadow.

Before her stood an apple tree laden with fruit. The tree called to her: "Please, young girl, pick the fruit from my limbs. My branches are breaking from their weight!" Quickly she did as the tree asked and continued on her way. Presently she came to an oven filled with fresh baked bread. "Oh, please, young girl, take out the loaves or they will burn!" called the oven, and she complied.

The girl went on her way until she came to a house deep in the forest. By the door grew a gnarled old elder tree with white blossoms and black berries. An old woman came to the door. This was Mother Holle, though the girl didn't know it. The old woman agreed to keep her as a servant if she would work hard, fluffing the feather beds and keeping the house clean. She did not know that when Mother Holle's feather beds are shaken in the otherworld, on earth there is snow. At the end of three years the girl asked if she could go home. I always wondered why, since she'd only be returning to a terrible stepsister, and to a stepmother who hated her. But such is the soulwork of a good girl. The soul likes to return to the familiar even if it was unpleasant to begin with.

The old woman showed her out by a different door, and as she passed under the lintel, gold coins showered down on her. She caught them in her skirts, and when she looked up, she found she was outside her own home. Needless to say, her family was impressed, and her stepmother thought it would be a good thing if her own daughter could make friends with Lady Luck in this way as well.

But when the stepsister came to the tree full of fruit and was asked in the same way to pick it, she did not stop, and when she came to the oven, she did not take out the bread. When she came to Mother Holle's house, she scarcely fluffed the pillows and swept the dust under the rug. When it was time for her to return home, she went out through the same door as her stepsister, but only tar and feathers showered down, and no matter how much she scrubbed, she could never get clean.

This is the justice of fairy tales. Good deeds get rewarded with good pay. Lady Luck is really an old woman with a long list of chores that you have to do.

Salvation is nice but good luck is better. I think that the endless desire of human beings to get lucky is the main reason goddess worship hasn't disappeared from the human psychic spectrum. We read fairy tales because somebody in them is always going to get lucky, and we want to know if this luck will be used well or foolishly. I have often wondered why it doesn't occur to those lucky souls who are given three wishes to ask first for a hundred more wishes! I would have done so. And then their wishes are often so silly. For example, the fisherman's wife wishes to be a king. What foolishness! Just wish for some great real estate! The rest will follow. To be a king is a job, when done well, not restful enjoyment. Who wants to be rich and isolated?

Fortuna, the gracious goddess of good luck, is the beneficent face of fate, Mother Holle on a good day. Fortuna has been in my face as long as I have been alive. She is often pictured on the front of homes in Hungary, or her small statue is placed in the gardens or in the middle of the yard. She is sometimes nude, but more often she wears a see-through chiton and her beauty shines forth. She looks like a lady who is accustomed to being treated very well, welcomed, never judged or criticized.

She is the giver of fun, music, parties, civilization, good health, money—and the one who enables people to win at games. Her special flower is the very common chamomile, not the rare rose, as one might expect. Gypsies always washed their hands in chamomile water before gambling in her honor. This herb cures colds; when inhaled, it cures coughs. It is a tranquilizer, a beneficent nervine, available in most grocery stores already made up in bags of tea. Lady Luck is also fond of cinnamon, which attracts wealth. Keeping cinnamon sticks in your coat pocket when gambling was another magical trick professionals used to use.

Lady Luck has been sung about in musicals, immortalized in common sayings ("Good luck to you!" "Luck be a lady tonight!"), and made the star in fairy tales. We all pray for health and happiness and money in front of our many altars. All religions promise some form of benefit to our lives. Thus, Lady Luck is still the focus of all human religions, without using her name. We all pray for good luck. We all thank the force for sustaining us. We all bless the divine will. All prayers, in all the various cultures and languages, are to the Fates. Who knew?

Where does she come from? The middle aspect of the Fates, whether you call her Verdandi (Norse) or Lachesis (Greek), survived the patriarchal ban on worship of the Fates by turning her into Fortuna. Renamed, given a face-lift, and separated from her sisters, she still rules today. We all know the Fates are the wealth specialists. When we buy a lottery ticket, who will decide the winning numbers? She who rules what is coming into being now!

Playing with the Fates in gambling is humanity's oldest way of engaging with these awesome sisters. From time immemorial, games of chance have been devised to choose winners and losers. Of course, life is a gamble as well: We choose a number; Fate decides if it will win. We choose a life; the Fates decide what kind of luck will affect it. Human beings have a deep longing to prove that they are lucky by winning something. Buying a lottery ticket is a chance to be part of the pool of people Lady Luck will play with. It is a license to dream. It is a way to lift up our spirits and imagine the unimaginable, the feeling of utter specialness. That's what a sudden change for the better can do to a human life.

But is that really what we want?

The girl who served Mother Holle received a shower of gold not by chance, but because she was generous and conscientious and had done her work without complaining. A few people are fated to have their lives turned around by luck, such as when a stroke of lightning hits, but most of us get along not by winning the lottery, but with help from our friends.

The Beatles knew that and sang about it. It's far wiser to ask the Fates for a helping hand than for the winning number. When friends help one another, they create a web of luck. The Fates understand webs and weaving. They love to weave in company. A helping hand can be manifested in the form of a great associate, a wonderful life partner, a move in your favor.

So far the Fates have turned a deaf ear on my prayers for the jackpot. But they have often sent me helpers. My true wealth is in friends. With friends, not only do you get to do what you want, but you have people with whom to share the goddess work and the rewards. Along with good health, there's nothing more precious to have!

The stepdaughter in the fairy tale helped the trees and the oven not because she expected a reward but because it was in her nature to be helpful. Being herself put her in harmony with Lady Luck, and so she was rewarded. By the same token, once you move into a synchronous relationship with the Fates, your luck should improve. But there are still no guarantees.

When it comes to healing, or good luck, Bona Fortuna is the female aspect of God who comes to the rescue. As our Lady of Guadeloupe or the Lady of Lourdes, the Mother of God watches over us even today. Versions of her have appeared under or in the Tree of Life, or at wells of healing and places of prophecy. You can't help asking, Is Fortuna the Mother of God? Only if God is lucky.

Summoning the Fates for Good Luck

The oldest, most heathen good-luck custom is to kiss your own hand while praying to the Moon. I am not kidding! This is a wonderful practice. It expresses self-love and total identification with the divine in an unabashed way. At first it feels silly, but once you get into it, you can generate a sense of self-esteem that goes sky-high. There were times when this form of prayer was outlawed by death. Kissing your own hand is a very old form of prayer whose origins are unknown. The European custom of kissing the hand of a woman must come from this. Kissing a woman's hand is kissing the hand of the Goddess.

While you are kissing your own hand, imagine the energy going to Fortuna, who is kissing your hand with your own lips. Ask for help with your own words. It is a good idea to have your own little self-made mantra, a little rhyme for luck. Think back; maybe your grandmother had a little rhyme you can recall. This you can repeat whenever you call on Fortuna. My own favorite example is:

> *Good luck that is needed, good luck that is speeded,*
> *good luck that is mine, come, now is the time!*

One way to get in tune with the Fates and pray for good omens is by making offerings, especially of alcohol. The ancient Greeks poured out wine for all their gods. Even today, rum and brandy are offered to Pele, the volcano goddess who holds the fate of Hawaii in her hands. When Pele threatened with volcanic eruptions, the Hawaiian kahunas poured bottles of high-quality rum and brandy all around the homes and property they were hoping to protect from the lava flow. The lava stopped where alcohol was given as an offering.

This act of pouring out alcohol is almost universal. In Hungary all *taltos* and wise women know to feed the sacred fire with wine and spirits, and sometimes with corn or wheat, and pray over them. Sacrifice of something of value is always part of any devotion. Whether the wine being sacrificed is defined as the blood of the moon or the sun, or of Jesus, the same idea is behind it. Wine is a transformational symbol; it is becoming, it is still fermenting, and drinking it alters our consciousness. Both the ancient Greek symposium and the Norse symbol were religious drinking parties during which people toasted the gods. Words mixed together with toasts to the moon or the sun or to a new happy couple constitute a blessing even today.

The Fates will enjoy their drinks, but if you are in dire need and really need to get their attention, legend has it you must sound a horn. Have you noticed how many religions use horns? The Tibetan monks blow horns, sometime made of human bones. The final battle of Ragnarok will begin when the god Heimdall blows his horn. The archangel Gabriel has a horn, and when it sounds rebirth time is near. Not the end of the world—just the opposite!

If you sound your horn, especially the ones hunters use, legend has it that Diana will wake up and rush to the sound. You can tell when she has arrived by the winds that strike your face, and by the sound of rustling in the trees. And you'd better have a prayer ready—she doesn't like to rush around for nothing. If she hears your prayer, the Fates will fulfill it.

Prepare for her by creating a small altar under a tree or on a rock or near water. Light herbs such as sage or bay lure and nourish the spirits. Diana (I use this name for the Fates since she is a triple goddess) is the soul of nature, so you must give her something natural to rest on. Even a glass of water would do if there are no flowers. Prepare a prayer that is short and to the point, and repeat it slowly three times. Here is an example:

> *Diana, ancient one, daughter of the starry night,*
> *Hunt down the enemies of peace and women.*
> *As you turn the wheels and shift the tides,*
> *The three old ones will shift the minds.*
> *The Fates will spin the wheel and cut the lies.*

If this is too lofty, make up a prayer that is closer to home, such as:

> *Diana, ancient one, daughter of the starry night*
> *Bring back balance into my body, laughter into my heart.*
> *As you turn the wheels and shift the tides*
> *The three old ones will shift the minds.*
> *The Fates will spin the wheel and cut the lies.*

Sound the horn again three times. Burn incense, which helps to carry the message to the spirit world. You don't have to give details to the Fates, only a plea for change.

CHAPTER TWO

ENTERING THE WORLD

Is the Dearest Goddess
a cuckoo bird?
This one gives
to some
too much,
while others have
nothing at all!

LATVIAN WOMEN'S FOLK POEM NO. 9163.88

The daughter of a friend of mine (I'll call her Carol) phoned the other day. "My mom said if I was in town I should ask you out to lunch," she said.

"All right," I answered, though I was a little puzzled. Most girls her age aren't so eager to socialize with their mother's friends.

We met for lunch, and by the time we got to the crème caramel, I was beginning to understand. Her mother had told her I am a priestess, and she wanted to talk.

"Z, I can't stop worrying. On both sides of my family I have relatives who have died of cancer, and I'm afraid I'm going to get it, too. It's so unfair! And then I was listening to a radio show and this man said we choose our own reality. But I didn't choose this, did I? Why did I have to get born into this family, anyhow?"

A good question. Should we blame ourselves when bad things happen or should we blame fate? Or is it all chance, anyway?

To understand who we are and how we got this way—and what the Fates have to do with it—we have to look back to our own beginnings.

CHOICE OR CHANCE?

Imagine that you can journey to the World Tree and see the gracious goddess Urdh, who is sitting there. She extends her hand into the great well of infinite possibilities, into the unknown. She pulls out a mass of unformed substance—could this be oxygen, hydrogen, and carbon? Maybe even she doesn't quite know what she's got there in her hand. This moment is pure chance, and chance is Lady Luck's middle name. Urdh works the substance in her hand into a true thread of life and begins to lengthen it, adding to it, twirling it, rolling it in her hands. Such is the picture of the first Fate goddess. Although her name, Urdh, and the word for our planet Earth come from different roots, to the modern ear they sound the same. And surely Mother Earth, Gaea, is a Fate goddess, too.

It is the Earth herself that spins the yarn of life, twists together the strands of DNA to make us what we are. From her deft hands we receive the gifts that have been passed down to us from our ancestors. She gives us our bodies—the most precious perfection we'll ever own. We are all born with a personal destiny comprised of elements of all that went before us. The cauldron of the human gene pool yields up our own unique combination. We get the color of our eyes, our body type and health, and our talent for artistic creation or the temperament that will help us to survive in the genes that we are assembled from.

As Urdh—that which has been—Mother Earth selects qualities from the genes of our ancestors. Will we be slim and tall or short and stocky? Pretty or smart or both? It is the past that also determines the nature of the environment, both physical and cultural, into which we are born. Part of that environment includes the personalities of our parents. Since opposites usually attract each other, we often have to integrate very diverse forces. Sometimes it feels as if everything is up to them, especially when we are power-

less as children. In German, *Ur* means something original, ancient—
the Urfrau, for example, is the original ancestor, the wild woman.

To talk about birth is to remember death. When you understand
the Fates as a natural force that encompasses the circle of rebirth,
you realize you have worried about the wrong god. These virgin
grandmothers cannot be changed. And they do balance the account.
It just takes them a while.

The other side of them is not that bad. Death, which they also
rule, is a melting pot of all that was alive and will live again. Death
becomes an exciting state, one existing between the worlds. It is in
flux. It is alive. It's Urdh's cauldron. Skuld leads us to fulfill our
potential in this life, and when we are done, we have to give back
the precious gift of our bodies, in which we have learned her lessons
and become part of Urdh's domain of history. The elements of our
bodies are recycled, and our spirits pass into Verdandi (Lachesis),
remaining there until we choose another life and become part of the
world once more.

Instead of thinking of death as a static, permanent state, we discover that there is nothing permanent about either life or death.
Only the dance of life and death and rebirth is eternal.

The Fates contain the majesty and mystery of death, and they
participate in the customs and the sorrows of the living. We offer
them our bodies when we are done and they take us back and down
and hold us in their good keeping. We bless them as the "good
ladies," the Gray Ones. They recycle us, and the unstoppable flow of
the life energy, the circle of rebirth, roars on.

Mother Earth gives us our bodies, but how do they become
connected to our souls? In Book Ten of *The Republic,* Plato tells the
following story:

> When all the souls had chosen their lives, they went
> before Lachesis. And she sent with each, as the guardian

of his life and the fulfiller of his choice, the "daimon" that he had chosen. And this divinity led the soul first to Clotho, under her hand and her turning of the spindle to ratify the destiny of his lot and choice, and after contact with her, the "daimon" led again the soul to the spinning of Atropos to make the web of its destiny irreversible. And then without a backward look it passed beneath the throne of Necessity.

When Plato described what happens between the worlds, he spoke of the soul as a major player. The soul is independent from the Fates, but in this time and space between the worlds, it interacts with the Fates; it is an equal partner. After the soul is united with a body, it carries out what has been chosen. But the soul is not alone. We each come with the guardian "daimon" (meaning "companion" in Greek), who will lead us to our lives and through it and afterward bring us back to where we first acquired its divine services.

Where is the soul between lives? The soul is a recurrent visitor in this realm of shades between the worlds. The soul rests here, sleeps here, exists here until it is time to move on to the wheel of life and choose anew. In the lap of Lachesis are all the choices. The soul could choose to be any creature that exists: a turtle, a deer, a lion, or a human being. If the soul wants to be human, it can choose male or female; it can even have an attraction to the prospective mother. But the soul is only half responsible for these choices; the other half will be up to the Fates. I don't think people choose unhappiness, but in this privileged realm between the worlds it doesn't matter if the life chosen is not destined to be all happy—reality is temporary, and all will return to the realm of the shades soon enough.

You could say that this "in-between" place, this "netherland," is the true reality. Its existence colors the reality we perceive, even though it is not of this moment. How can two worlds exist side by side, affect each other so powerfully but still be separate? In nature it happens all the time. The moon never touches the earth, but her magnetic field affects the growth of grass, hair, nails, and many other things. When the moon is waxing, things tend to grow faster; when she is waning, growth slows down, wounds even bleed less.

But if the soul has a choice about its incarnation, why are so many people born into unhappy lives? That's because the soul has more important things than comfort to pursue. The soul has a mission. That mission is to help the Fates make all things pass (which is a huge job!)—to make history, to advance the development of the human race, to create the future as it should unfold, and not least, to complete its own evolution. This purpose is best fulfilled when we choose a life that supports the mission, that spurs on the soul to grow into its destiny. In choosing our lives, we are partners with the Fates. This timeless time, this place in between the worlds—here we are totally, authentically ourselves.

The rest of our incarnation consists of the gradual unfolding of this all-important prebirth choice. The physical and psychic attributes that will enable the soul to fulfill its purpose come from the parents the Fates and we choose. The Fates place us in a situation in which we have a chance to manifest the purpose, the mission, for which we chose to incarnate.

Once the soul has chosen a life, Lachesis (Verdandi) takes us over to Clotho, who will touch it and make the choice irreversible, then begin to spin her thread. Atropos weaves the life choice to fullness. Then the soul is passed under the throne of Necessity and dispatched to the river of forgetfulness. There it stays for a time, drinking in great big gulps. This slowly erases all memories of past lives, all memories of the Fates and the fateful choice of ours. According to Hungarian lore, eventually the north wind picks us up and carries us into our mother's womb.

After this we feel only the yearning need to remember what we are supposed to do, and the agony if we think we have forever forgotten. One of the needs of the soul is to connect to the universe often during our lifetimes in order to stay well. This we do through touching life by loving one another and our own bodies, and by loving nature through animals, gardening, and simply being outdoors. Prayer, ritual, and simple acts of acknowledging the divine can bring us back from the brink of loneliness.

But don't worry, the Fates have not forgotten us. They spin out our thread and we make our choices. Our talents, such as aptitudes for our line of work or art, have already been bestowed on us. If we know what gifts we have been given, we can guess at what we are supposed to do with them. If you have a great voice but are color-blind, you cannot change to become a great painter. If you are not a maternal woman, you should not be pressured into motherhood. Choosing to be female is not the same as choosing to be a mother. Some women are not meant to bear babies. But more than enough are.

Plato tells us how the soul decides what its purpose in life will be, but who is the soul? Is she separate from you? Is the soul the true you? Is the soul superior to the body?

The soul exists before your body is conceived, abiding in the netherworld, waiting for a chance to be embodied. "Time" as we know it does not exist in the place where souls await the opportunity to slip into a fertilized egg. We have seen this place of waiting in the many inspired religious paintings of the Blessed Virgin Mother, surrounded by weightless little cherubs, many of them flying. The laughing, fat little figures hold up her garment and suspend her crown over her head. These are the unborn babies surrounding each fertile young woman. Like a small group of faithful souls, they hover around us, hoping to be there when one of our eggs gets fertilized. We are born with thousands of eggs, many more than we need to bear a few children. Nature works out of abundance.

The soul enters the body at conception. Is this the beginning of life? It is the beginning of the body, but not of the soul that animates it. Life was preexistent. The soul comes from the Divine Source. It is part of the evolving individual until the body dies. The body is an equal partner in each incarnation. It is the visible side of the soul.

Urdh reaches into the cauldron of infinite possibilities and catches the little soul. With her hand she unites the threads of the body, its matter, with the substance of soul, which is ethereal, and creates the thread of life. Even a moment of drowsy desire can open the door to conception. Four o'clock in the morning when the train goes by and wakes up a couple just long enough to connect is a good time. The souls watch the sleeping couples in the wee hours. They wish to be there when the conception occurs. Some friends of mine have actual memories of waiting for their turn, climbing up a ladder and then leaping from the top with many other children behind them, leaping into the darkness of the womb.

If the mother is not able to open the door of life and give birth and care and love to the newborn, she may choose abortion. She may make this choice in order to invite the soul to try a better mother, or a better time, or she may do so because she chooses not to be a mother. The soul is not destroyed. It goes back to the source, the primordial cauldron of Urdh, where it can wait in bliss until the right time to come back and take a body.

There is no need to be angry at those mothers who choose abortion. It is only the physical vehicle they are rejecting; they have no power to harm the soul, which is eternal and lives with the Goddess.

Mother Nature in her infinite wisdom has given women the power and the responsibility to bear the young, and it is a woman's responsibility to determine whether she will be able to fulfill that trust. Mothers often report that they feel that the soul of a child who died or was aborted has returned in a later pregnancy, a few more mature years down the line. For the souls waiting there is no time.

More people are embodied today than ever before. Some have baby showers and vitamin pills and many family members and birthday parties. Some have nothing to eat, and filth, violence, and sickness await them. The soul leaps and both the fortunate and the disadvantaged are in the Fates' hands. All things must pass. We are "staffing" the times for the Fates.

CONCEPTION RITUAL

If you are trying to conceive, you can consciously call on the Fates to aid you with the following ritual, using one of the oldest fertility symbols, the egg.

The egg is a major symbol of fate. Think about all the rituals we have already that include eggs. In the old days when audiences didn't like a performance, for example, they threw rotten eggs at the stage or at the unfortunate fellow on it. What were those eggs saying? Breaking eggs on somebody along with a bad wish (get off the stage!) is a hex to make the Fates stop something.

But the use of eggs in protection spells or good-luck rituals is even more common. Think about the Easter egg hunt. The eggs are decorated, glorified, made into little works of art, imbued with thoughts and wishes and fun. The colors on them are equally mean-ingful: Blue eggs bring love, red ones health, pink ones happiness, white ones blessings. The practice of decorating eggs goes back at least to the fifth century, and some of the patterns used in Eastern Europe are even older. In the ritual hunt for hidden eggs, we inter-act with the Fates by allowing them to direct our steps. Then chance, or alignment with the pattern of fate, enables us to find them.

To perform a spell for conceiving a child, select three fresh eggs. Make a nest for them with an herb called verbena, or, if you are of Italian descent, you may want to use *ruta* (or rue). These herbs are sacred to the goddess of fertility and ward off evil. Decorate the nest, then put in presents for the new baby such as little hearts, sparkling stars, etc. Paint or dye the eggs red. Write on them the names you would give your baby, for both a boy and a girl. Take these eggs and the nest out under the full moon and light three red candles around them. Pray to the Fates in hushed tones, whispering on the winds:

> *Come, Urdh, release the new soul to be my child.*
> *Come, Verdandi, sprinkle me with the waters of life.*
> *Come, Skuld, and bring what must be.*
> *I bless the Fates!*
> *I bless the three Fates!*
> *I bless the three Fates!*

Now hold the eggs in your hands and say:

> *Mine is the power of the Goddess,*
> *Mine is the blood that grants life.*
> *I am calling on the new soul to enter,*
> *I am giving the new soul life divine.*

After the ritual, make love outside in the moonlight if you can. If not, go inside and make love there. In the ancient poems about Inanna, the goddess tells her lover to "plow my earth thrice." So you should make love three times that night for good luck. If you are using donated sperm for artificial insemination, bless it three times under the moonlight before you take it inside your body, saying:

> *Bless this sperm, oh Moon,*
> *Bless it with strength, health, and power.*

Leave the eggs outdoors, where some animal will receive the offering on behalf of the Goddess. If you bring them home, keep them under your bed, and when you have conceived, give them to a stray dog to eat. Dogs are sacred to Hecate of the crossroads. She is another triple goddess, known as a fate goddess, priestess of the fourth. To her, hounds are sacred and feeding stray animals brings good luck.

The Guardian of the Soul

As was related in the excerpt from *The Republic* quoted earlier in this chapter, a being the Greeks called a "daimon" facilitates the soul's passage into the body and environment into which it will be born. The daimon is our companion, our familiar, our guardian angel. From now on I will use the term "guardian angel" because it's well known to all of us who have paid attention to soulworks.

We meet our guardian angel before we are conceived, when we are pure destiny, pure soul. It is a divine being, an eternal one. We have the angel to protect our lives and help us to achieve our goals. She prompts us to articulate needs that must be fulfilled, and to whisper the oath with which we bind ourselves. The angel causes the restlessness that makes us change, plots the "accidental" events that move us in the right direction when we are turned around, thinking of other things.

It is this angel who recognizes people from earlier lives, especially lovers and mothers and other blood relatives. How often do we feel we have known a person before? This familiar feeling makes you trust the person immediately and take chances with him or her. You surrender to the feeling of trust via love. This is another skill of the angel to make us change.

Sometimes the angel whispers the warning or slows the steps that save a life, like the time I was late for the massacre. Often since then I have wondered why I lived and all those other people died. Sometimes I've felt guilty about it, and at other times I've felt a responsibility to do something important with my life to justify having been saved. Many of us can remember a time when we missed death by a hair, when we knew survival was a miracle. We have these feelings whenever there is a disaster. We watch in awed horror as the evening news shows pictures of an airplane crash, or of an earthquake. It is hard to believe that all those people, especially little children, somehow "deserved" to die. It has taken me a long time to put such disasters in perspective and come to some conclusion about them that makes sense to me.

I am still learning about the Fates and how they work, but it seems to me that the problem is in the way we look at death. If we have only one lifetime, then the greatest good is to live as long as possible; thus, a life cut short is indeed a tragedy. But if the spirit lives on, either in another state of being or by being born into another body, then a shortened life may be a misfortune, because the person was prevented from learning all that being alive in that time and place had to teach, but it is not a disaster. What you don't learn in this life, you'll learn the next time around. Why does this seem so hollow when we lose a beloved to death? Because those left behind are not in bliss, they are in deep grieving. But only life hurts.

The Fates weave our life threads in and out. Sometimes the thread breaks and has to be knotted together, and sometimes the weave gets a bit twisted, but the overall pattern continues to grow. Your guardian angel knows what your place in the pattern should be. Her sole job is to look after you. The more clearly you learn to work with the Fates and understand your destiny, the easier it will be for you to hear their soft whisper of warning or sense a funny feeling you get in the gut. If you listen, you will be protected. If you tempt the Fates too much, well, even an angel can snap, and you'll have to start over.

Witches acknowledge this being as the "familiar" spirit, the kindred spirit, the soul guardian, and teach that we can work with it to fulfill our destiny. All things have their guardians, even the corners of the universe. We each have a companion from the spirit world to help us get and fulfill our destiny. As soon as we light a candle, we summon this spirit.

Sacred technology requires that all the senses be represented in prayer—scent, touch, sight, taste, and hearing. The guardian then connects us to the great all, the Flow of Life, the energy river. We draw power, energy, from this wonderful river of life when our angel is activated to bring us help. It appears that no matter what religion you practice, if you pray to your "god," your healing spirit gets activated. Ultimately religions are star-born. They change as the great ages change, slowly and deeply. Calling on the spirit is the eternal religion.

The angel holds the knowledge of who we are supposed to be. As we journey through life, she releases knowledge to us a little at a time—not more than we need, and not sooner than we need. To progress, we need the stimulus of an active spirituality. James Hillman compares the soul to an acorn that holds the code for the growing oak tree. In spirit we already know who we are and who we will become. It is only the manifestation that takes time.

But is it enough to simply allow what must be to happen, without our active participation, or is there a moment in time when we can hold destiny's hand, as a child holds his mother's hand while crossing the street?

The concept of "crossing over" is important to an understanding of fate. We use this expression for death, but we could just as well think of birth as a crossing over into the world of the living. "Death" implies an ending. "Crossing over" carries the image of movement toward a larger reality, like "going overseas" to a distant but pleasant place where another life will begin.

We will have many little psychic deaths, or crossings, during our lifetimes. Birth itself is a death for one stage of life. Living in the womb was a paradise, the last paradise we will know for a long time. The fetus dies and an infant is born. These little deaths bring us emotional maturity and wisdom. They illuminate our possibilities, dislodge us from places we've grown too fond of or too unhappy in. They bring us grief . . . and happiness. The part of you that hurts when something ends is the part that teaches. The hurt will stop in time. The teaching remains.

The threads of life cross over one another and create new patterns. We are the woven and we are the web. A good thread surrenders to the Fates' direction in the weaving. Surrender is saying yes to the new.

Urdh has given each one of us our angel, a spark from her own breast. Learn to listen to her and she will keep you on track. She leads the soul to Verdandi and Skuld. She knows where we have come from and where we are going, though she keeps her knowledge of the future in shadow, where we will not be able to see it until we have gone by. The exception is, of course, divination. Here we have a chance to take a glimpse into the open book of energy.

DESTINY AND KARMA

"Janet, what on earth happened to you?" I exclaimed. For a minute I wasn't even sure the woman I saw looking through the bin of oranges in the supermarket was my friend—a big bandage covered half her forehead and she had a black eye.

"Oh, my karma really caught up with me this time!" She smiled ruefully. "A pickup truck ran a red light at the intersection of Broadway and McArthur just as I started through, and when I tried to keep from hitting it, my brakes failed and I banged my head on the edge of the steering wheel. Do you think maybe in a previous life I ran over someone?"

"No way!" I said, thinking it was more likely that she'd tempted the Fates by not having new shoes put on her brakes when she was supposed to. Common sense was missing. The Fates don't like that.

Janet was notorious for not keeping up with basic maintenance of her automobiles. The last time I rode in her car, the door handle fell off in my hand. After that, I decided my own karma didn't include intentionally putting myself in the way of an accident waiting to happen, and refused to drive with her.

"Well, be sure and get plenty of rest," I said when she wound down. "Karma is action that shakes you up, whatever its cause."

Since the sixties, the word *karma* has become part of our vocabulary. "Instant karma gonna get you," John Lennon warned us. But how few of those who use the word so freely actually understand it!

Every choice we make has consequences. Karma does not mean that some misfortune must befall a person to punish him for something he did in another lifetime. That is a reactionary and false assumption. Lifetimes are separate from one another like beads on a necklace. There is no carry-over guilt. There is no carry-over punishment. All things conclude at death. Only the living carry on consequences. Only the living inherit the past.

New Age religions often explain away their lack of social responsibility by citing karmic justice. If events are destined to happen, why bother to change things? However, abused children, as well as the brutalized victims of revolutions, wars, and assorted violent acts, are not suffering from bad karma. They do not "deserve" mistreatment in this life because of bad deeds done in previous lives. While being abused may not be a destiny, being born into patriarchal times and woman-hating cultures, for example, in which violent acts are rampant, may be a soul's opportunity to fight injustice.

Why do bad things happen to the innocent? This is a thorny question. People always want explanations for evil and pain and sickness and disaster. I don't have the answer. Nobody does. But why don't we ask equally why the good times come, why are we healthy? Why do we have fun and live well? Why is there love and luck? The good and the bad are part of the cosmic soup that bubbles in Fate's cauldron. Life contains birth and its own destruction. When you start a new life, you deal the best you can with the historical realities it brings you, whether they are wars or bad parents. Karma can be instant or snail slow.

What matters is not so much what we are given as how we deal with it. In this glorious little niche is the free will's power. We choose how to respond to adversity, or not to respond at all. Some would say that even applying your talents is destiny. What if you don't have any talents? What if you are an average person with no special gifts at all?

And yet in nature there is no such thing as "average." Nature makes no judgments. If you are well and alive and having a good time, you are a raving success. Nothing more is required from the life of a human or an animal or a tree; just be, and be well. Revel in the ordinariness of it all, and when you die, submit and do it gracefully.

"What goes around comes around!" is a phrase with which I have often consoled myself when injustice happens to me. "She'll get hers!" "Her turn will come!" The voice of wishful thinking assures me that an avenging angel has been dispatched to serve me. The long arm of the Fates is supposed to rectify wrongs; the Furies are to wipe the earth clean of evil.

Guess what? The Fates don't do details. Wiping things off the Earth is not their beat. They only do the big picture, turn the wheel of the ages, and facilitate our souls' choices. The Fates don't create evil. Evil is a perception from our point of view. It belongs to the small picture. To us it is overwhelming, but cosmically it is the bat of an eyelash. It is a knot, a rough thread in the Fates' hands, but they don't tangle it. Despite everything we can do to snarl up the works, they turn the wheels and keep everything moving, flowing, spinning. Surviving.

So where does evil come from?

Evil comes from the times, the collective human consciousness, the level and kind of civilization. There is no outside devil; the devil is always internal. The content of our times, even the darkest of thoughts, originates in us. We in turn are a product of what we know, and thereby lies the choice: to learn or not to learn. If you explore and inform yourself abundantly, chances are you will make heartfelt, soulful choices. But there are always those who won't: too lazy, too dense, our opposites.

Karma implies action—we have done something, made a free choice, made a move, and now it has consequences. This result of our action is karma. Contrast that with falling in love with your best friend's wife or husband. You really truly wish it hadn't happened. It's terrible, you feel guilty, why couldn't you fall in love with somebody more suitable? Because falling in love is not karma, not a choice; falling in love is not under your control. The Fates arrange love. Destiny brings people together for many purposes. To facilitate a destiny shift, or to love again some soul from our past. Falling in love always feels otherworldly. It's directly from between the worlds, where the wheels within the wheels converge, led by the divine spark from the bosom of Verdandi. At first it may seem an accident, but later it looks more like an elaborate scheme, when a tiny change in the schedule, a tiny allowance to chance, results in dramatic life changes.

A Western woman who is used to a staggering array of options would loathe going through life without making choices. We are mad for karma; we love choices, love to create consequences. It makes us feel as if we are in control of our lives. And to a degree we are. Just not as much as we think. We are still doing details. We can see how the Fates create the big picture and, in consultation with the soul, decide what qualities we will bring into this world, but they don't tell us what to do with them.

That is our business. So long as we live we can revel in free choice. In tight spots we can call the Fates to help us, but asking for help is a choice that itself helps to put us in alignment with karma. Karma can smooth out the rough edges of destiny. We can be born into poverty but work our way out of it and end up rich. We can be born rich and throw it all away, killing ourselves with drugs. Was it destiny to be poor, or rich? Did poverty motivate us to achievement, or did riches destroy our will? Destiny and karma intertwine and often support each other.

I am reminded of the days when I was studying theater improvisation with Second City in Chicago. In one of the exercises, we were told who we were, and where we were, and what we wanted, then let loose to improv it out with one another. Because there was no script, often quite unexpected things came out of the exercise, just as they do in real life. Those unexpected moments were treasured. I can still hear the voice of my teacher, Viola Spolin, calling out, "Let the moment teach!"

Life is an improvisation. The Fates set up the situation and introduce the characters, but they leave the decisions on how to play them up to us.

I tried to explain some of this to Carol that day when we met.

"You're looking at your family and thinking you're going to die, but you know, so is everybody else. The first thing to consider is that you have some warning about how. And you could be wrong. There are a lot of other things that could happen before then. Does that sound depressing? What I'm trying to say is that really you're no worse off than everyone else. Take precautions. Get regular checkups and eat right. But beyond that, don't let the fear of death ruin your life!"

I suggested that she think about the positive reasons that she might have been chosen to be born to her father and mother. What good things had she gotten from her family heritage?

"You are what you are!" I told her. "You can't just take some parts and reject others. In a different family, you wouldn't be you. You're alive now, so live! Life and death are part of a cycle, and right now it's living that you have to pay attention to."

And then I talked a little bit about the guardian angel—the daimon—and how she could learn to work with her to fulfill the purpose for which she had been born. By the time we left the restaurant, Carol seemed much more cheerful, which made me feel good, too.

She had asked a hard question, and there aren't any easy answers. We don't "make our own reality" in the sense of arranging for bad things to happen to us. But my study of the Fates has convinced me that we do have a part in choosing the kinds of challenges we'll face, and we certainly are responsible for deciding how we will meet them.

WORKING: DREAMING THE ANGEL

Understanding what is going on with your life mission and what to do about it is a lot easier if you have a good relationship with your angel.

In European folk tradition there are many spells for a girl to undertake in order to foresee who she is going to marry. This rite is an adaptation of that. Whether it works on men, I don't know, never having tried it, but it can have interesting results in the world of the spirit.

The rite should be performed on a night that is a threshold of some kind—between the seasons, between the years, or even Sunday evening, the beginning of the week. Traditional dates are Halloween, New Year's Eve, May Eve, and Midsummer's Eve. You will need an apple.

Apples are a favorite fate symbol. In the Bible Eve eats an apple, a fruit from the tree of knowledge. What knowledge? you may ask. Good and evil? Is that all? How about the origin of all life? How about the knowledge of how the universe works? How about the knowledge of past lives? Those are the true forbidden, mysterious fate sciences.

In Scandinavia, a goddess called Idunn kept an orchard where she grew the apples of immortality that kept the gods young. In fairy tales the apples are often golden and grow on fairy trees. Apples can be poisoned, as in the story of Snow White, and then they bring death. Witches used apples in love spells. You write a letter to the Fates in the apple when you enclose your wishes in it. After casting spells, witches toss apples into the wilderness for the wild animals to eat as thank-you notes to the Fates for success.

At midnight, take the apple and, standing on the threshold of your house, cut it in half. Say:

> *Between the days [or between the seasons, the years, etc.]*
> *I stand,*
> *Life lies in my hand—*
> *Half for what is outside, half for what's within;*
> *Half for what is coming, half for what has been.*
> *Thus I divide what once was whole,*
> *That I may see my secret soul!*

Lay one half of the apple outside the door, and take the other half, wrap it in a handkerchief, and place it under your pillow.

Before you go to sleep, ask your angel to send you a dream that will tell you something about how you can become more aware of your destiny. Put a notebook and pen beside your bed, and as soon as you open your eyes in the morning, write down as much as you can remember about your dreams. Take both halves of the apple to a park and leave them there without looking back.

It may take you a while to understand what your dream is saying, but as you meditate on it, gradually a meaning will emerge. You can try to contact your angel again through dreams (without the apple) and other forms of meditation. Eventually, especially if you do the other workings in this book, you will be able to hear.

Urdh

Chapter Three

Urdh

Here I am
wishing to be
this,
wishing to be
that.
Before I dare
wish for more,
let me see
how
the Dearest Goddess
endowed me.

LATVIAN WOMEN'S FOLK POEM
NO. 38633.322

This is the beginning.

It is New Year's Eve. I draw three circles around myself for protection, since interviewing Urdh, who rules all that is past, is scary. But where there is fear there is power.

On my altar, white sage is burning in a new incense holder in the form of the three Graces. I am wearing the Fates' colors, a black-and-white sweater with a red crocheted poncho over it that my mother gave to me. I light a white candle, which has already been blessed by being used in a ritual to Brigid, another Fate goddess.

I come fasting and rested, fresh from a long, relaxing bath. Outside, the wind is singing spells on my wind chimes. I sink back into my comfortable chair.

"Dearest Urdh!" I whisper. "Hello! Or should I call you Earth? Maybe Gaia? The first Fate."

The dog scratches at the door. I sigh and get up to open it for him, but Zoro just stands in the doorway. I realize then that I have opened the door not for him, but for Urdh. Zoro heard better than I did.

"Spirit of Wisdom, please allow me to welcome you!" I see no one, but I can tell that she has come in. Her answer comes to me:

"I see you have put out my favorite things. Eggs, flowers, a picture of a spinning wheel on that postcard. But I think I will abide in your clock—digital clocks are so restful; no more of that endless tick, tick, tock."

So we sit, the Goddess in my clock and I in my chair.

"So, what's new?" I finally ask.

The first Fate looks at me with her invisible eyes and says inside my head, "I live in the world of the past. You are new, living in the changing now. You tell me."

"Well, in the here and now it is New Year's Eve."

"Ah, this year is almost back in my lap," she cries. "I bury all things, fold them back into the good earth, gather them into the past. At midnight everyone feels my presence. They kiss each other in my honor—the only time your culture lets strangers kiss each other."

"Kissing is good for people," I say.

"Kissing is important for the Fates as well. When you kiss you make life connections. It's like a powerful electrical current that runs from you to us."

To please her, I kiss my own hand, as we do in the old Hungarian custom of greeting the new moon. *"Uj hold, uj kiraly!"* (New moon, new king). The warmth of my hand is like life itself. It never occurred to me that that could be such a pleasure.

"The Goddess is pleased as well. Kissing your own hand three times is the old way to call me."

"Nobody kisses their own hand anymore, Urdh, even in your honor. We would feel foolish. Lovers kiss each other, and women get their hands kissed sometimes, but no one kisses their own. It's the times. Nobody understands the Fates anymore."

I feel movement and suddenly I can see her, wrapped in dark draperies, with an urn balanced on her head. Behind her is a deep well. She goes to it and fills her urn with beautiful clean water, then picks it up and comes back to me. With even, wavelike movements she sprinkles the water over me and on the ground.

"They may not understand us," she replies, "but they pray to us, in every earthquake, every hurricane. People use different names, but we know who they mean! Remember the Cold War, when you lived in fear of nuclear annihilation? The clock was ticking then—it was five minutes to midnight. Everybody prayed to us then! But it wasn't your destiny to be wiped out, and so you were spared."

The first Fate looks awesome when she is passionate, a ghostly bride from ancient times, veiled in cloud and speaking with the tongue of the spirits, so softly I have to strain to hear.

"You would all have less trouble if you would remember more often to kiss your hand to me," she says. "We use your hands to create, and think with your minds. The kisses that touch your hand land on the Fates' blushing cheeks."

> *Everything that is mine is thyne*
> *Everything that is thyne is mine*
> *Tout tout throughout and about!*

This little ancient rhyme lodged itself in my brain. Now I have a special rhyme to go with this identification with the divine spell.

She scoops out a hole in the moistened ground, ready to receive the year that is almost past.

Good-bye to 1996! It has been a rich year for me. Urdh wraps it in her veil. It keeps it contained, she says.

I loved this year. I didn't fry in the summer or freeze in the winter, and was sick only once, with the flu. I had lots of good times and got to stay close to home. And almost daily I prayed to the Fates upon the winds.

As the digital clock shows midnight, Urdh unceremoniously drops my year into her deep hole and lovingly covers it with moist earth.

Now it can grow! But first it must sleep. . . .

And the new year is released from beneath her many skirts, insubstantial and waiting to be filled, and flows out into the waiting world.

PLAYING WITH THE PAST

Urdh is the first Fate, the one who looks back at what has been. In the old stories, when only one of the Fates is mentioned by name, it is usually Urdh. Our ancestors knew that the present is built on the foundation of the past. Situations don't pop into existence out of nowhere—they are the results of long chains of events in which many elements from the past combine. Even the choices we make in the present are conditioned by what has been done to us and what we have done before.

But, you may say, the past is past—what can we do about it now?

You may feel like a completely different person from the little girl whom the other kids teased on the playground, or the teenager who suffered when her parents divorced, but she is still alive inside you. As you read about the significant fate dates of childhood and adolescence, you may wish you could have had these ceremonies then. You can't go back in time, but you can awaken your younger self and give her what she needs.

And of course if you are a mother with children, you can honor their transitions with rites of passage.

BIRTH BLESSINGS

In this all-important act of naming, we play with the Fates once again, because the name of the child will call up images in the minds of those who know her; the name will become her identity. The French psychologist and philosopher Lacan built an entire system of psychology based on the associations produced by different names. Often people display the qualities that their names suggest—is this the influence of the name, or was the name given because the parents sensed the child's character? When a child is born, the name the parents had been intending to give often seems inappropriate and so they choose another. Children who are given the wrong birth names often feel it and change them when they are grown.

The ancient Norse understood this. In the "Lay of Helgi Hjorvarthson," a poem in the Elder Edda, the hero is "large of body and handsome. He spoke little, and no name would stick to him." He spends his time sitting on a hill, fit only to watch the sheep and considered by his noble family to be a half-wit. One day nine Valkyries, supernatural warrior-women who are related to the Norns, come riding by. Their leader, Svava, calls the boy by the name Helgi, the hallowed one, and tells him that the eagles who cried out at his birth prophesied that he would never amount to anything if he didn't speak.

Receiving his name transforms the boy into a hero. He asks Svava for a gift, as was customarily requested of the person who "fastened" a name on someone in that culture, and insists that she herself be part of it or he will not accept the name. Traditionally, a Valkyrie could attach herself to a hero and function like Plato's "daimon" as a guide and protector. Svava is both a human woman and a magic being, and becomes both his lover and his helper. In later poems, both he and she are reincarnated several times.

In some traditions the child is given two names, one that is the secret name of the soul, and the other a name by which the child will be known to the world. The naming ceremony blesses the mother and the child together. The naming is a way to bind the child to the new world; the secret name is to protect the soul. The soul name is known only to the mother and father or to the godmother. It will be used again at the next rite of passage, when the child reaches puberty and moves from her first destiny to the next. At this point, the child may be given a new soul name.

A formal naming ceremony invokes the Fates as an immediate presence and helps bring child and parents into harmony with their purposes. The Fates are very close at the time of birth and during the first few months. The naming ceremony is when the good and bad fairies visit to make their wishes for the newborn.

The fairies who give gifts to the newborn are a staple of medieval tales. Traditionally there are twelve of them, who line up to bestow their blessings.

"I'll give her the generosity of her grandmother's heart," says one.

"I'll give her the mathematical capabilities of her grandfather," chimes in another.

"I'll give her a love of music."

"I'll make her able to draw."

But there is always that thirteenth witch, who was not invited, the shunned fairy, the fate goddess who arrives last and gives us our challenge.

"I'll give her a patriarchal culture to grow up in! I'll put her in a time when the media will tell her that her body is ugly! I'll give her math anxiety! I'll give her hard choices!"

WORKING: NAMING CEREMONY

In a naming ceremony, family and friends can take the part of those powerful spirits, engaging positive energy by their good wishes, and perhaps persuading the attendant Fates to follow the crowd! The Fates will appreciate being honored with ceremony and ritual.

Create a small altar either in your home or outside under a tree. It should hold flowers of the season and offerings of fruits and grains, such as barley for prosperity, oranges for health, flour for domestic happiness, and salt for wisdom and protection against bad things. In the middle place three fresh eggs, the favorite symbols of the Fates. Paint the name of the child on the eggs, both the secret name and the public one. Many female names are goddess names or represent positive qualities. In Hungarian, for example, the name Emese means storyteller or dreamer. In English, Diana is a popular goddess name, meaning Holy Mother, Lucy means light. Any book of baby names will give you more ideas. Even if the baby's public name is significant more for family reasons than spiritual ones, her soul name can be chosen for its symbolism.

Set out thirteen seats and invite thirteen friends (the number thirteen is for the moons in a year). Each guest represents one of the Fates and gets to bless the child with a wish. You will have a more balanced set of blessings if you discuss the possibilities beforehand. Twelve of the guests should wish for blessings, and the thirteenth should appease the Fates by wishing for a minor flaw. She has to bring in some shadows.

You may begin by having one or both parents talk about the things the baby inherits from each side of the family, both physical qualities and traditions, and the environment into which the child has been born. If you know an astrologer, have the baby's chart interpreted. This tells everyone what the Fates have given the child already.

Sprinkle the child with a little flour, barley, and salt to keep her safe and prosperous and wise. Sprinkle water on the child three times, the Fates' number. This symbolizes the life-giving waters of Urdh's sacred well, which Verdandi and Skuld pour on the roots of the World Tree every day to make it grow and keep it eternally strong. Then announce the child's public name and whisper the soul name into her ear. Give the child to each of the thirteen guests in turn to hold while the blessings are given. If you don't have thirteen people to invite, try nine, or three, and arrange for some of them to give more than one blessing.

When all the "gifts" have been given, bless the food you eat and sit down to dinner. The feast should include magical dishes containing

barley, flour, and salt, and figs for sexuality, round pastries for pleasure, breads and vegetables for health, beets as a protection against
disease, and garlic to banish sickness. Once these requirements are
fulfilled, the menu can feature whatever foods you like best.

During dinner toast the mother and the child together, not just
the child alone. Subsequent toasts can cover additional blessings:
"May the Fates bless you with a sense of humor!" "May the Fates
bless you with wisdom!"

When the dinner is over, the community will have received a
magical soul reincarnated, complete with name and destiny.

CHILDHOOD: ENCOUNTERING THE WORLD

The restless years of childhood are full of magic. Study your own
childhood and you will see already present the shadow of your destiny. What did you want most? Go back to it, explore it. What was
it like to run, learn, paint, tell stories? Only now do I realize how
many of the things I enjoyed as a child became grown-up passions,
although rarely in any way I might have expected.

I always enjoyed the rituals the Catholic Church had in honor
of Mary. As a child I always loved the Mother of God. Who would
have thought that thirty years later I would be one of the first
women to return the Divine Feminine to a position of popular
reverence among women? My friend Eva and I spent many summer days collecting, smelling, drying the flowers we would later
throw in front of the priest as he carried the statue of Mary. But
we, too, would have the pleasure to walk on those flower petals
ourselves.

My love for ritual was fed by exposure to the ceremonies of the
Church, the familiar bells calling us to prayers at regular times. The
pious little girl who honored Mary grew into a goddess-loving high
priestess and witch who has changed the world by sparking the

women's spirituality movement. Walking on rose petals can do that to a girl.

When I was six years old I played at being a priestess. I built a temple out of red bricks, smeared herbs on its walls, and installed reluctant insects in it for worshipers. Since I was an only child, I learned how to populate my world from my fertile imagination. This was most beneficial because later as a writer I could stand the long lonely hours of the profession better. I think as children we know where we are going if we are left alone enough to focus on our inner life. It is the interior life that holds our life's goals and answers; we can intuit them better when alone.

My sons also displayed interests that suggested their destinies at an early age. Gàbor loved to examine the heavens for stars. He saved all his allowance to buy a good telescope in order to view them better. Astronomy was his first science; later he extended his interest to biology, the cosmos at a cellular level. Today he is a scientist. My older son, Làszlò, loved to build airplanes and rockets. He got his pilot's wings before he got his driver's license, and today he is a pilot for TWA. The Fates use childhood experiences as building blocks for the first destiny. (The first destiny is from ages 1–29 years old.)

Who were you when you were growing up? Go back in your memory. What were your favorite toys? What kind of games did you play with others, and even more important, how did you amuse yourself when you were alone? Can you trace a relationship between those childhood passions and the things you love now? If not, think about your life more carefully and explore the possibility that when you left childhood behind you may have left an important part of your soul as well.

You may still find yourself restless, prone to open up doors you are not supposed to open, make decisions you later may or may not regret, make mistakes, make good moves. Children are naturally perpetually restless, often to their parents' dismay. Even as adults, we can recapture childhood's energy by allowing ourselves to experience that dissatisfaction with present conditions, that tireless curiosity.

Cherish restlessness, especially if you find yourself growing complacent. Restlessness is not the same as anxiety, though the symptoms may be similar. Anxiety comes from fear of change; restlessness seeks it. Change is the means by which the Fates make us grow. They want us to change, move on, change again and again until the incarnate individual is a true expression of the immortal soul. If we resist change and refuse to play with the Fates, they lose interest, and we cease to grow. The shuttle gets stuck between the threads and we become the background instead of the pattern.

FATEFUL BIRTHDAYS OF CHILDHOOD

As we move toward adulthood, we mark our birthdays with excitement and celebration. But in terms of the work of the Fates, some birthdays are more significant than others. These are the auspicious times, when rituals and celebrations should commemorate the changes.

What are some of the important birthdays you should look back on?

Age three is a magical time. It's when the soul surfaces for the first time and looks out at the world, and it should be celebrated with "extra" ceremony. At this birthday the soul reveals its purpose. A three-year-old is often wise beyond her age. We say the darndest things then; we are truth-sayers. We haven't yet learned to hide our authentic selves for the sake of others.

Children are often asked what they want to be when they grow up. I remember being put on the spot when I was three. My answer was, "I want to be a guest." "A guest!" they cried. "That's not a profession!" But I had noticed that when guests came everybody was nicer; my parents brought out the sweets; they paid me more attention. My parents treated honored guests better than they did each other, so it looked like a good thing to be.

The interesting thing is that my fate has been to be a guest quite often—a guest on the Earth, then a guest in other countries. These days I give lectures as a guest speaker. Even at the fateful age of three the little person has an ancient soul that already knows where she is going. When asked, the child may actually, prophetically, foretell the general path ahead.

At the age of three, Roseanne, the famous TV star, played at being a star with her own show named *Roseanne*. Her sister Geraldine brought in the other little kids in the neighborhood to watch the show. Roseanne knew she would have her own TV show even then. My own sister, writer and journalist Peg Jordan, remembers a vivid train ride to California when she was three and sat in the dome car, pretending she was the engineer of the train. She knew then that she would live in a beautiful place in California someday and have a wonderful life but that she would have to endure all sorts of hardships first. I know a little girl named Tara who, when she was three, always knew when the moon would rise. When it was imminent, her little face would light up with mystery and she'd drag her parents outside to view it. She would watch for a long time, saying, "Look! Moon!" I wonder if she will turn out to be a spirit healer because her soul was so happy to see the moon. Or she could be an astronomer discovering new stars. Time will tell.

The seventh birthday begins the time of initiation into the spirit world. On this date, acknowledge the child's spiritual nature by giving her more exposure to mythology and religion; a new sacred name may be given as well, with the appropriate rituals. Remember when you were seven. Did you experience a sense of the mysterious, the divine? If you did not have an elder to initiate you, did you have a spontaneous awesome experience? Helen Keller was seven years old when she met Annie Sullivan, her legendary teacher, for the first time. She opened up her life and brought her the destiny to be a healer.

The fourteenth year marks the first half of the Saturn cycle. It is time to go to work on some important project of great interest. It's either that or hormonal hell. By now, the menstrual cycle will probably have stabilized, and if it was not done earlier, female relatives and friends can arrange an initiation into womanhood by celebrating the first blood. If you don't want to make a lot out of this celebration, lighting a single red candle with your daughter on the eve of her first blood is enough. Sit down with her and tell her your truth and share the story of your own first blood with her. Your lighting a candle for her new womanhood will signify your respect for the young woman she is becoming.

At fourteen a boy should be well into puberty, and will benefit from an initiation-into-manhood rite, perhaps a camping trip, with his father and friends. (Much more on this in my book *The Holy Book of Women's Mysteries,* in the chapter "Sacred Sons.")

WORKINGS: COMING OF AGE

The next fate date is nineteen, the completion of the first fertility cycle. A young woman of nineteen named Sally once came to my friend and fellow priestess Diana and asked her for a ritual to celebrate her coming of age. Sally had been taking care of herself since she was fourteen, and in every way that counted she was an adult, but she felt the need for a formal ceremony to confirm her womanhood. Yes, these things also happen to young women even in the depth of patriarchy.

Diana gathered a group of women and they had a ritual. Sally loved it, and later it was repeated for many other young women. The basic structure is as follows:

Invite a group of female friends to celebrate with you. Try to have women of all ages present, and ask one of them to act as the leader. Ideally, do this ritual at a home with a hot tub, but if that is not possible, decorate the bathroom with flowers, incense, and candles.

The celebration begins with a ritual bath. Draw a bath, then get in the tub and wash away your old self, using a scented soap such as sandalwood or lavender. If there is space, some of the other women can dip up water with shells and pour it over you. This part should last about half an hour and be performed in total silence. When you are ready to emerge from your purification, submerge yourself totally underwater and when you come back up say your new name. For example, Sally shouted out, "I am Towanda!"

When you have been dried off, put on a new garment—a loose robe or caftan works well. The other women should be wearing loose, colorful garments also.

All of the women stand in a line and each one embraces you as you pass, saying, "With this embrace I welcome you into the circle of womanhood."

Then everyone sits down, the older women on one side, the women who are married or established in life on another, and the women just starting out on a third. If you want to get really fancy, they can wear robes or waist cords of black, red, and white, respectively. You sit in the center and wear white.

Light candles for the Three Fates. Then the women from each group share their experiences of what it means to be a woman at each stage of life. The conversation can get very frank here and often very funny.

When all have spoken, they bless you and give you gifts, and then everyone feasts. All this can happen in an imperfect world even if it's just one evening long.

WORKINGS: SPIRIT NAMES

"So," you may say, "this is fine advice for those whose mothers are reading this book now, but for me, those birthdays were a long time ago."

True, but that doesn't mean you can't still celebrate them. Here is a ritual you can do for the girl who still lives within.

Spend some time thinking about names. Have you ever had the feeling that the name that identifies you to the world is not the right name for the real you? Or that you have more than one personality—perhaps the person you are at work and someone else who likes to run along the beach or listen to music? Choose a name for that free spirit, the real you. Then have a party to which you invite those friends, be they many or few, with whom you want to share this part of yourself.

Get your favorite kind of cake and put on it seven lucky candles. After everyone has arrived and you have socialized for a while, light the seven candles for the Fates who have invented the first seven letters of the alphabet and who watch over you. Then have the whole company chant your new name seven times so it sticks.

OUR FIRST MISSION

"What were you like when you were twenty-one?" I ask my friend Diana.

"Hmm. When I was twenty-one I graduated from Mills College," she says. "I loved Mills. For the first time in my life I was around people who cared about the same things I did. I found out what I liked and what I could do. I was healthy and bright and reasonably good-looking, though I didn't think so at the time—who does? When I marched away from the stage with my diploma in hand I felt completed. I had finished turning into my grown-up self. I thought I knew exactly who I was and what I was going to do with my life."

"And did you?"

"No, of course not, or at least not at all in the way I expected. I don't suppose I'll ever again be as certain about anything as I was about myself then. What about you?"

I laughed. When I was twenty-one I already had two children and thought I would spend my life as a wife and mother. I was mercifully wrong, too.

Age twenty-one is a major fate date. You become a legal adult, with all the rights and responsibilities (though most of us don't think about that part) that go along with it. At this point you are three-quarters of the way through your first Saturn cycle. You may think of age twenty-one as a beginning, but in fact it is a "graduation." The term comes from the Latin word for "a step," and when we come of age, we are moving from one step to another on the first flight of stairs of our life. And yet it is a spiral staircase. Some steps are higher than others, and from time to time we can pause, but as we go up, we go around and around, revisiting the same places at a higher level than before.

The twenties are the years when we create the first self. At the age of twenty-one you may think you know exactly who you are and what you are going to do with your life, and it is true. This is, however, only your first self, who will be the mother of the person you become after your Saturn return. This is the first flight of the soul, when she looks around for connections. It is a time for making sense of the past, balancing the books. Urdh, keeper of the unborn, is still very close. The first cycle, from one to thirty years, is under the keeping of Urdh. In it we fulfill the mission we inherit from the past. Whether we follow the track on which we have been set by our parents—finishing school, starting an approved career—or whether we rebel against our upbringing and become political or cultural revolutionaries, our first mission is shaped by our history.

By the time we reach our twenties, education has opened up our minds and we can see the bigger picture to which we belong. We are filled with goodwill, a yearning to make the world a better place. We feel immortal; we think we know everything. We are ready to serve life, make commitments; we are passionate about a lot of things.

We are dead certain about love. We want it. We feel it. In our twenties, fertility has us by the soft thighs. There is no better time for us to create new people than now. Our eggs are healthy. Our bodies are bursting with cosmic energy to connect with old souls and create the future.

People ask, "What do you want to do with your life? Where are you going to live? How will you make your money?" Many twenty-year-olds are still in school, custodians of the cultural heritage. Many have to work, custodians of the responsibilities freshly assumed. Many get married, have babies, drop out of school, become wives, mothers, custodians of the future. Are we still in the race? Is this when we become our own parents? Not really. It's just our first destiny.

The first destiny blooms in the twenties. The teens were a time of discovery; during the twenties it is time to plant the garden—our first garden—which is very special indeed.

Somebody ought to tell the people in their twenties not to worry. In our twenties we have acquired our first clues about what life is all about and we are in a hurry to rush into it, mostly following plans that other people have made for us. But *relax;* you are not even grown up until you are thirty. So go ahead, risk and learn.

My heart aches to see young people marching into the work force like little clones, looking thirty-five at twenty-five. I see their young eyes already resigned, their spark sacrificed to the spirit of duty, seeking status and money. Some swear they'll be millionaires by the time they're thirty. Maybe money will set them free. At thirty the treasure you need is not money. The currency of youth is time. Freedom. Leisure. Passion.

The Industrial Age has taken away our soultime for passionless jobs, but the Information Age is arriving, and it's time to unwind.

What you do in your twenties can prepare you for the work you will be doing later on, when again you are asked to create something out of nothing. Going to college or just taking classes, reading books, traveling without a goal—are all great ways to gather the treasures that will become your stimuli or simply your memories, part of who you are. If your love of life leads you into a career or if your passion is touched off by a cause, give yourself to it freely.

Youth is resented in our culture at the same time that it is outwardly worshiped. It is not young people themselves who are being worshiped, just their youth. Young people are feared when traveling in groups on the streets. They are not rented to; they are discriminated against; but they are always envied. It is not good for society to resent their young.

When I was a student in Vienna, people who learned that I was going to the university treated me with respect. In previous times, young people would leave the ancient village and embark on their "wonder" (meaning wandering) years. Students traveled from town to town looking for their destiny, a mentor, something to learn, something to excel in. Older people helped them, fed them, put them up at night because somewhere their own kids similarly benefited from the hospitality extended to youth. When they returned a few years later, they were welcomed back, given a place. They demonstrated their specialty and were recognized as masters, with permission from the town to practice.

Without that support, people in their twenties can be the most lonely folks on earth, desperate to be loved, to be appreciated, to belong. As a result, some join cults that promise a community. From ages seventeen to twenty-seven there is a great yearning to show up the old folks for the fools they are and join a group of people with whom they can share life and purpose.

Young people also need to be alone for the shy soul to be heard. Introspection is healing, soulwork at its best. Some kinds of exploration happen alone, and some kinds happen with others. Young people reflect one another like mirrors; they learn about themselves by comparing, contrasting, bouncing ideas off one another. Youth has to mass, swarm, herd, and flock together at sports events, festivals, dances. The individual soul develops alone, but it is together that the group mind of a generation strengthens.

We need to revive the old seasonal revels, the ribald traditional festivals of the turning year. We need the celebrations that involve the entire city or nation. The measly handful of national holidays we have today are not enough. We need more processions in the streets—for fun, in order to disrupt the humdrum progress of daily life. We need the playful cross-dressing that relieved tension between the sexes, the masked balls at midnight, street clowning, ritual role reversals, folk theater, and folk dances. Celebrations are political in the sense that they unify and feed the spirit of the polis, the community.

There is a season for every natural event. On the wheel of life, the twenties are equivalent to Easter. At the spring equinox we should have great dances, create ways that single people can safely meet one another. The festival whose name was retained for the Christian feast of the Resurrection was originally a celebration of the resurrection of all life in the spring—the rising of the sap, the return of the birds, and the return of love in human hearts. Shut down the city for block parties, let young people meet their neighbors. We need to create a culture of the Earth in which youth can feel protected yet free.

When the soul reaches her twenties, she is wise to her environment. She understands survival. Blessed with a body that is young and strong, she is ready to fall in love with life. Her feelings are strong as well, for the young soul still remembers the bliss of the place between the worlds, and still has a great capacity for ecstasy. The work of the soul at this time is to allow this flowering without judging it, if the surrounding culture permits, and if not, to take a daring risk. Now is the time to take on a big challenge, to make history for Urdh to remember.

If a nation's twenty-something generation is not rebellious, it is in big trouble. The future will be as stale as week-old champagne. The twenty-year-old is emerging from the past (Urdh) and creating, however briefly, something new for the world. This emergence is exciting; the hands of the Fates are almost visible in their lives. Any country that doesn't have students marching for freedom is doomed. Society always has room for improvement, and it is the young who are best at finding out what to do, what to change. What is wrong with our world? they must ask. What do we need to do about it?

Each generation has a task, determined by the movement of the planet Pluto through the signs of the zodiac (see chapter 10). The young manifest history. They create the new sagas, put the energy behind the next turn of the wheel.

IDENTIFYING YOUR DESIRES

In the twenties, introspection can be turned to the examination of our desires. Desire is the Fates' way of showing us which way to go. It is a complex process. We can only say yes to each of its twists and turns until it settles down, and looking back, we can see for the first time destiny's clue. But only at the end of the process will we be sure. While we are in the midst of it, which is most of the time, we can only keep saying yes to the goal that draws us. The rest will follow.

At twenty-one we have created the first self, our first being. From here until the first Saturn return, at age twenty-eight or twenty-nine, there are few landmarks. It is as if at this point in our lives the Fates are easing up on us, leaving more room for us to make our own decisions. Make mistakes; get experience.

All we have to do is engage the new self with the world. How, in what way we do it, is up to us. There is no way to do it wrong. We can revel in free will. Life is a kind of breathless free fall of events, anyway, inner and outer intermingled. What checkpoints can guide you?

Ask first, Where is your desire? If nobody was trying to push you in other directions, where would you go? If no threads bound you to the wills of others, if money was no object, what would you do? And how much do you desire that goal? There is a subtle interaction here between free will and our Urdh destiny. Whatever we do will have some relationship to the past, because what we bring to the present are the skills and information and desires that Urdh has given us. The trick is to find a first mission that will fulfill the promise of the past, rather than confining us to the past's limitations or compelling us to rebel against it. But rebelling is good.

The next point to examine is urgency. What feels as though it has to get done right away? What thoughts push into your head when there is nobody else to think about for a little while, when you are alone with yourself at last?

Urgency, fear, anxiety are all high-octane fuel for the passions. Your future is mirrored in your present. What makes your heart pound with excitement? Listen to your body, for it carries clues to your destiny. What you learn from your body is important. If you feel physical excitement at the thought of things that don't fit into your life right now, perhaps you should take it as a challenge to incorporate them as you can.

The soul's job during the twenties is to find you a first mission in life. This will be easier if you do your part. Have you found a worthy goal? Has your heart turned toward a cause that needs your help? Peace is a popular goal. And there are never enough who are truly willing to work for it. Only in peace is there wealth for all. The earth, the oceans, the forests, the mountains, and the deserts all need the passion of the young. There is so much to protect. This is soulwork translated into action. Sometimes picking up garbage on the street is a high form of prayer. Investigate everything. If there is enough exposure to options, the soul will pick out her own destiny to follow.

Once your higher purpose is found, you will feel it. It's a tingle, a rising excitement, the heart beats faster. The soul recognizes destiny's clue and will affect the body. Watch your reactions. Are you lit up? If so, pursue the goal that made you feel this way.

We usually notice this feeling when we fall in love. When fate leads us to someone who makes us feel this special way, it doesn't always mean sexual excitement. Sometimes it's just a recognition that your soulmate has arrived, the special somebody with whom we have a lot of soulwork to do.

When the goal of the Fates is revealed, we must surrender to it. Surrender is not easy nowadays. We are taught to control everything, fix all problems. But life is not to be fixed. It's a web. The pain and unfixed parts are lead threads to show the soul the direction. Surrender seems like weakness, but it is just the opposite. To surrender you give up the controls to the invisible hands of the mastery of the Fates. Trying to manipulate them only slows things down. If you don't change when they first suggest it, they'll fill you with restlessness and stimulate your sense of desire until they catch you with your defenses down.

Some of these events are often perceived as reversals and as such are hard to accept. Sometimes they make you think you have wasted years studying the wrong subjects, getting the wrong diploma, missing the boat in your choices. But even apparent disasters can teach you something; they make you stretch. Nothing you have ever done is wasted. And even when the action of the Fates in your life seems most chaotic, they are still working. You cannot miss the proverbial "boat" of life. The fates are unavoidable.

WORKING: THE DOORWAY OF DESIRE

What if you don't know what you want? Nothing attracts you, it's hard to get up the energy to pursue any goal? Here is a spell to strengthen your desire.

Get a red candle, as bright as blood. With a pin, or the point of a nail file, mark it off into seven equal sections, and scratch the word

YES into the wax in each. Physical actions such as this communicate your will to your unconscious as well as to the cosmos.

Breathe on the candle and say, "May the power of air awaken my desire." Sprinkle it with water and say, "May the power of water purify my desire." Take a little olive oil and sprinkle a few grains of salt into it, then use it to anoint the candle, and say, "May the power of the Earth feed my desire." Then light the candle and say, "May the angel who guides my soul kindle a desire in my heart that will lead me!"

Gaze at the flame until it fills your vision. Feel the heat of the fire burning through your veins. Take the flame of desire into yourself until you feel it burning in your heart. Let it burn down to the first mark.

Repeat this process for six more nights, until the candle is all burned down. Now release the power of the spell into the universe by taking the bits of wax that remain and throwing them into running water or leaving them at a crossroads. Turn and walk away without looking backward to allow the spell to leave you, and return fulfilled.

WORKING: HONORING URDH

What if you need to deal with the role that Urdh—your past—has played throughout your life in making you the person you are today?

For this, you need to do an adaptation of the ritual for celebrating a birthday. As a rite for Urdh, it can be done at any time; the candles are not for you but for the Goddess.

Urdh's color is black, because the past is in shadow. For the ritual, you will need a black cloth to cover your altar, and as many short black candles as you have had birthdays (you can cut tapers in quarters or thirds). You may want to wear black as well. If you need some moral support, invite a friend or two to sit with you, but be sure they are people to whom you can tell everything, or you will not be able to take full advantage of Urdh's teaching.

Take a large tray, or cover a big piece of cardboard with aluminum foil, and make candleholders from the foil for each candle, then set them on the tray, making sure to leave enough room between them so that they will not melt one another. Better yet, you could stick the candles in a tray of sand. You will also need matches and a long taper for lighting the candles.

Prepare for the ritual by refreshing your memory on the dates of important events in your life—when you entered a school or left it, jobs, moves, injuries, disasters and accomplishments, the beginning and ending of relationships. Bring your notes with you.

Make an altar to Urdh, covered with a black cloth, on which you place items symbolic of your past—a family tree, your birth certificate, old ID cards, photo albums and yearbooks, newspaper clippings, pay stubs, even IRS returns. These are only suggestions. Find a statue you like and wrap it in a black veil.

Light some myrrh or sage incense, and carry it clockwise around the room. Declare that this space is now the temple of Urdh, to which you have come to receive her blessing.

Then sit down and light the first candle. Say the year of your first birthday. Aloud or silently, meditate on all that you know about your beginnings—your parents, your birthplace, your family's origins. Then ask Urdh if there is anything she wishes to teach you. Sit in silence for a few minutes, opening your mind to her wisdom. Then write down whatever has come to you. (Or tape the whole session.)

Year by year, light the candles, paying special attention to the years representing your fate dates, or in which you can recall events of particular importance. Obviously the older you are, the longer this will take. Eventually, however, you will have lit all of the candles. As you watch them burn down, contemplate the shape of your life. Ask Urdh to show you the patterns, the connections; allow her to teach you how your past has formed the person you are now. This teaching comes to you in meditation, or "accidentally," later on.

As the candles burn out, let those years go. When they are all finished, thank Urdh for her gifts to you and throw a veil over the altar. Take the candle stubs and melted wax to a living body of water, put them in, and leave without looking back.

After you have performed this ritual, eat and drink to restore your energy, then go to bed. Keep a notebook handy and when you wake up, record your dreams. This ritual is even more enjoyable if witnessed by your friends in the context of a birthday party.

A Spell for Letting Go

At certain points in your life you may find it necessary to consciously let go of the past. The Urdh ritual described above may dredge up memories you have repressed or forgotten, which you now need to release so that you can go on.

Find a small object that symbolizes the element in your past that you need to let go of—a doll, a favorite blanket, a toy or a ring, a letter, or something similar. It should be something that will hurt a little, but not be extremely painful, to give up. Take a walk one evening to some spot outdoors where you can have some privacy—a park, say, or the shore of a lake or the sea. Burn the object, or cast it into water that is alive and flowing. Say:

> *Blessed be Urdh! Mother of the past!*
> *I give you this gift symbol of my youth*
> *Good-bye to my childhood, I loved you well.*
> *Thanks for the blessings!*
> *Blessed be Urdh! Mother of the past!*

Offer red apples to the Fates by casting them where wild animals will be able to find them.

Cast flowers to the four directions for the blessings that will come. Close your eyes. Turn your body in place. Then jump, and when you land, you'll find yourself in Verdandi's garden.

JUST ANOTHER LEARNING EXPERIENCE

Dance, Marsha,
dance.
Take
no worry.
Your Dearest Goddess
guards you.
Your Dearest Goddess
sits
in a silver boat
and wears
a golden
crown.

LATVIAN WOMEN'S FOLK POEM
NO. 11696.324

Our lives are made up of a series of challenges. We manage to get through adolescence, sure that once we are "grown-up" everything will be fine. We work our way through school, look forward to graduation. Then the search for a career is on, and about the time we've settled into that, we hit the first Saturn return! Just when we think we have everything settled, along comes another "learning experience."

This cyclical pattern in life is reflected in folk tales, which are rarely simple and complete stories. Instead, our hero or heroine lives through one adventure after another. The story that follows is about a Hungarian lad called Marci. I invite all the women to see themselves in this character because Marci stands in for us all. His adventures may be more colorful than ours, but surely they are no more serious than those we all face as we go through our first destiny.

Once upon a time there was a very poor woman who had a son named Marci. This boy was a very honest, decent young man. In addition to having a reputation for honesty, people also said that he could do just about anything that he set his mind to. Inevitably, this information reached the ears of the king.

This king was of a very jealous nature. It seemed to him that if people compared him to young Marci, he would come out the loser, so he sent for the boy, with the hidden purpose of tricking and then destroying him.

And so Marci came to the palace. When they met, the king said, "You're famous, you know. They say you can do anything. So prove it. But if you can't do what I ask, your head will be off your shoulders before you can sneeze!"

"What do you want me to do?" Marci asked.

"I have twelve workers plowing my fields with twelve oxen. Steal those oxen!"

The boy was astonished at this, but he answered, "Your Highness, I have never stolen anything, and I'd rather not—"

"Then your head will be off before you can sneeze. On the other hand, if you succeed, I'll give you all my treasure. It's only fitting, since I stole it all myself!"

Marci nodded sadly and went home. When he told his mother what had happened, she shook her head in disbelief.

"Think hard, my son," she said, "think very hard!"

Marci thought hard. Then he smiled. "Mom, could you get me twelve snow-white chickens and one black hen? I have an idea."

His mother got him the chickens, and Marci carried them away and let them go just at the edge of the fields. Then he called out to the men who were plowing.

"Look! It's the wild black hen with her snow-white chicks! If you catch them, you'll have good luck forever!"

When the plowmen saw the black hen and her chicks pecking in the turned-up dirt, they dropped their oxgoads and ran off to catch the chickens, leaving the oxen standing in the field. The chickens fled into the woods and the plowmen disappeared after them. When they were gone, Marci took all twelve oxen and their plows and drove them home.

The next day the king called him back to the palace. He was not pleased.

"I hear you have successfully stolen my oxen and my plows," he growled.

"I did," Marci agreed. "Would you like them back now?"

"You took advantage of a bunch of fools," said the king. "Before you get your reward you must steal the grain from my silos by morning. It will not be easy, for it is carefully watched, but if you fail, your head will be off before you can sneeze!"

"And if I succeed?"

"If you are equal to that task, you get my entire kingdom. It's only fitting, since I stole it myself."

"Well, I'll try. . . ." Marci went home, wondering how he could steal all that grain from the big silos of the king.

The king was not taking any chances. He spoke sternly to the men who were guarding his silos, warning them of the boy who had already stolen his oxen and plows, and gave them a couple of slugs of whiskey from his flask to make them like him more.

"And give the boy a hard beating while you're at it!" he said as he went away.

When Marci heard about this, he smiled again. Then he made a straw man that looked like him, putting his own clothes on its limbs and his own hat on its head. He set it up near the silos, and then, though it made his head feel loose on his shoulders, let out a big sneeze. Well, the men watching the silos came out to see, still a little tipsy from the king's whiskey, and proceeded to beat the straw man until there was nothing left but chaff. They marched off to report their victory to the king, and he gave them more whiskey and let them sleep on his floor till morning.

This gave Marci plenty of time to steal all the grain.

That morning he sent his mother to tell the king that he had completed his task as promised.

The king turned red in the face from anger. He ran to see the silos, and indeed there was not a grain of wheat remaining. He called Marci to his castle once more.

"Marci, I have one last challenge for you. In my stable is a fine stall, and in that stall is a golden-haired horse, and a hundred servants who are watching over him. If you can steal that horse, I'll give you my crown, as is only fitting, since I stole it myself. If you fail, your head will be off your shoulders before you can sneeze!"

Marci went home again, thinking hard. He dressed up as a beggar with a bottle of brandy under his arm and knocked on the stable door. But the servants had been warned, and at first they refused to let him in. Then he showed them the bottle.

"It's only an old beggar," they told one another. "What harm can he do?" And so they let him in.

Once inside, the beggar man offered his bottle to those in his company, as is the custom, and soon the servants were all drunk. But even when drunk, one servant was holding on to the tail of the golden-haired horse, another held the bit, and a third was sitting on its back! By now the others had passed out, and soon the three who were hanging on to the horse fell asleep, too.

Very carefully, Marci made a tail of straw and placed it in the first servant's hand. A basket handle replaced the bit. The one who was sitting on the horse was more of a problem, but after a little thought, Marci simply uncinched the girths and lifted him off, saddle and all. Then he led away the golden-haired horse and took it home.

In the morning, the king went down to his stable, certain he had won. But the beautiful golden-haired horse was gone!

"You good-for-nothings!" he yelled. "Is this how you watch over my horses? The golden-haired horse is gone!"

"But I'm still holding its tail!" cried the first servant.

"I'm holding the bit!" cried the second.

"I'm sitting on it!" the third man yelled.

Then they got their eyes open and saw that they had been tricked.

The king was dancing with anger. Despite what he had promised, he now decided to give one more challenge to Marci and destroy him. He thought long and hard. Then he summoned Marci, who thought he was going to get his reward at last.

"Those tests weren't fair ones," the king told him, "because you were up against underlings. Steal my dinner from in front of me, and I'll believe you can do anything. If you succeed, you'll get my sword, which is only fitting, because I stole it myself. If you fail, your head will be off before you can sneeze!"

This really was a challenge, but at dinner, when the food was being served, the cook called out that a hand was poking through a crack in the floor of the kitchen. The king cried that it must be Marci and ran to the kitchen to expose the culprit. The hand turned out to be made of wood. And while they were gone, Marci swept the dinner off the table and took it home to his mother's house, where they feasted well.

But the king still couldn't accept defeat.

"I want you to steal the wedding ring off my wife's hand!"

"What will you give me if I succeed?"

"The princess in marriage, and that's only fitting, because she was the old king's daughter, not my own! But if you fail, your head will be off before you can sneeze!"

By now Marci was getting accustomed to his new profession, and he agreed. Besides, he really liked the princess.

That night Marci hid near the king's bedroom, where he could hear the king talking to his wife.

"I am going out for a little walk before bed," the king said. "When I get back, give me the ring. It will be safer with me."

The king went for his walk, and he looked very carefully about him, you may be sure, in case Marci was there. But there was no one to be seen.

In the meantime, Marci was stealing into the bedroom. Changing his voice to sound like the king's, he told the queen, "Darling, you'd better give me the ring now. That damn Marci could be nearby!"

The queen handed him the ring in the dark. Then he stayed near the door, and when the king opened it on his return, he slipped through it and ran away.

The king took off his clothes and got into bed. "All right," he said to his wife, "now give me the ring!"

"How can I, when I gave it to you only a few moments ago? You asked for it, and I put it in your hand!"

The king was so angry now he could not even speak. But too many people had heard his promises to Marci, and he could think of no more tasks to give the thief.

So Marci and his mother went to the castle and claimed the kingdom, the sword, the crown, and the treasures from the king, as well as the princess, who had liked him from the start.

Now, that was a wonderful wedding. They feasted on the finest foods and drank the finest wines and danced until dawn. Everybody had a joyous time, and even the gypsies were served coffee. And the three old aunties from the village danced their lucky three rounds of dance with their knees pulled up high. This brought excellent luck, they said.

In this story there are five tasks, five challenges for the honest young person. All of them are disreputable deeds, but they must be accomplished. To me, the king represents the patriarchy, which tries to corrupt the young by forcing them to do deeds that are as dirty as ones they have done themselves. The king himself acknowledges that he stole the kingdom, the treasure, the crown, and the sword—and even his daughter isn't his own.

What is the significance of the items to be stolen? There are five items, a pentad of things, that a young person needs.

The twelve oxen plowing the fields stand for the twelve months of labor during a year. All labor is symbolized by the patient oxen; ancient allies of humans, they are steadfast and obedient, and a means of production. To steal them, our hero uses the common belief in Fortuna, the Fates, Lady Luck, to distract the workers. The black hen and her white chicks function as a kind of Hungarian leprechaun. To catch them brings luck and treasure. The poor workers cannot let a chance like this slip by, and so they abandon their posts.

The second challenge is to steal the grain from the silos. In many folk tales the hero has animal helpers to accomplish this task, but Marci does it by using his wits, which is one of the reasons I love this tale. The grain is a symbol of survival; it sustains life, protects against starvation. A young person has to take power in society, get his share of the goods.

The straw man is not Marci but his specter. In this episode, the young person learns the difference between what the world sees and his true self. Marci has a healthy self-image. He knows the straw man is false, but he is clever enough to use it to tempt the blind anger of those who hate, and let them rip up his "image" and walk off with the grain while they are still trapped in their false reality.

The third item he has to steal is the golden-haired horse. In Hungarian mythology, the horse can fly; it is the *taltos,* the soul of the nation. This image must have come from the experience of racing across the plains of Asia. In Hungarian folk tales horses are always magic, but in this one, the horse is a captive. It simply stands there while the servants hold on to it.

To release this captive "soul," Marci has to disguise himself as an old man, a beggar, another traditional character in fairy tales. The old man holds wisdom, but what the servants accept from him are illusion and alcohol. The brandy gets them drunk, even though they still think they are doing their job. With their senses confused, they fall asleep, and Marci, using his wits, again takes the treasure.

Marci now has the means of production, the produce, and the soul—energy, matter, and spirit. What more can be required?

The king's dinner stands for the civilization built by the old. The meat, the wine, the bread are the products of a developed culture, the inheritance of the next generation. But the king isn't ready to pass it on. The false hand that distracts him is youth's ability to apply its power.

It is significant that Marci brings all his prizes home to his mother. In this story the two of them are close; they work together. In such tales the female principal of the universe is usually represented by the queen, but here she is the mother of this clever boy.

But the queen also has a role to play. The last thing a young person needs is the ring of relationship. This is a special ring, because it is the symbol of the king's link with the queen, his claim to power. She passes it to the young man in the dark, bypassing overt conflict, depriving the king of his sovereignty. This is life. The ring, the princess, and the queen all represent union with the source of life and love. The boy finally achieves it by eavesdropping on a private conversation. He breaks boundaries between young and old, becomes the king's shadow, understands him.

By stealing what had been stolen, Marci in a sense restores it. He already has won all that makes the king powerful. When he marries the princess, he and she become king and queen; the younger generation replaces the old.

This is what you have to do to claim your place in the universe. These tasks are the business of the first destiny, the first thirty years of our lives.

CHAPTER FOUR

FIRST SATURN RETURN

The Dearest Goddess
gave me
a thousand songs
at the tip
of every
wheel spoke.
Whenever
I'm sad,
all I need
to do
is turn
the wheel,
and song
flows.

LATVIAN WOMEN'S FOLK POEM
NO. 35817.83

There's a café called the Gaylords on Piedmont Avenue in Oakland that I like to visit after I've been walking my little black dog, Zoro. There are wrought-iron tables outside in front, so I can tie Zoro up right by me while I eat my salad. They will even give me an extra bowl so I can give him water. The café is a favorite lunch spot for the young women who work in the boutiques nearby, and I like to listen to them talking.

"Jo, I don't know what's happening to me! Last year I finally got my life together, and now it's all coming apart on me again. . . ."

The speaker looks as if she is in her late twenties, with smooth, short dark hair. Her friend Jo, who has curly blond hair, leans forward. Around her neck is a pendant with the astrological sign for Aquarius. That attracts my interest, since it's my sign, too.

"You just had a birthday, Mira, didn't you?"

"What does that have to do with it? I'm not even thirty yet——"

Jo laughs. "No, you're twenty-eight, and you're going through your first Saturn return."

Mira frowns. "I think I saw something about that in *Marie Claire,* but I'm not into astrology, so I didn't read the article."

"It doesn't matter—the stars don't care if you believe in them, they change you just the same. Saturn is like an old witch stirring her cauldron, and now she's in the same place in the sky she was when you were born, so it's your turn to be stirred."

"And how long is this supposed to last?" Mira asks skeptically.

"Oh, you'll be done by the time you're thirty—probably." Jo grins. "You know, they say the most dangerous time in our lives is around twenty-seven or twenty-eight."

"Why is that?"

"Most of the suicides happen around this age."

"Not me!"

At that point the waitress comes with their check, they pay her, and get up to go.

"Oh, what a cute dog!" exclaims Jo as they go by my table.

"Yeah, Jo," says Mira, "he's got dreadlocks just like yours!"

They stoop to pet Zoro, who bounces up and tries to lick their hands, and then, still laughing, they go on their way.

Good luck to you! I think as I watch them walk down the street. Your friend is right. Twenty-seven and twenty-eight are the most dangerous years. It's the time when one Fate, Urdh, is handing you over to the next Fate, Verdandi. In this limbo many things can happen. Very deep lows and very high highs. If Saturn has a grip on you, whether you like it or not, things are going to change!

JUMPING BACK INTO THE CAULDRON

At the end of your twenties, the planet Saturn takes you through the first astrological initiation into adulthood. Pay careful attention. When this is over, you will have claimed ownership of your new life and shared power with your destiny. You have to do all that and earn a living as well.

Your Saturn return will rock your world. Saturn is the mother lode. This huge galactic entity has to do with maturing, establishing, power, discipline, longevity, purpose, wisdom, and growing up. The changes she brings, like the contractions of labor or orgasm, involve some major energy!

Saturn's movements rule the slow but deep personality changes we experience as we mature. Each time it returns to the natal point in our birth chart, another initiation occurs. This planet is often misunderstood, described in astrology texts as a masculine energy, a taskmaster, a restricter of freedom, and a cause of scarcity and obstacles. To me Saturn is the great teacher and grandmother of personality, as well as the one who helps us make a living. She connects us to the outside world yet trains us to deal with the world within.

Saturn rules the following aspects of our lives:

1. Psychic stability. Everything in our lives depends upon good mental health. Our perception of the world, our ability to feel joy, our capacity to feel and return love—all these are part of a healthy psyche.

2. Public image. Saturn influences what we think we want to prove to the outside world. This can be difficult, since we develop such a compulsion to prove ourselves when we are growing up. Ultimately we must temper this ambition with self-knowledge and self-approval.

3. Personal expectations. Saturn helps to determine what we demand from ourselves. This is where the idea of Saturn as taskmaster comes from. What we demand from ourselves is often what we demand from others, but others may not have the same needs. We have to learn to have reasonable expectations both of ourselves and of others. Still, we need this drive in order to make a living.

4. Values. Saturn influences our decisions about what we value, what we will preserve no matter what the cost. Our character develops out of our values.

5. Respect. Because we are drawn to others with similar values, Saturn determines what qualities we respect in others. This is a very important influence, since it determines whom we choose to associate with. Shared values motivate us to join social groups, parties, causes.

We need Saturn's influence, but it must be tempered with flexibility. The things we feel threatened by, or whose loss tests us, are determined by saturnine influence as well. Many things can stimulate this fear, but serious illness or loss of loved ones ranks right at the top. Feeling threatened is being vulnerable to fear; the antidote to fear is information.

At this time of our lives our first task is to become aware of the divine essence of the soul. Who are we? Why are we here? The purpose of the human organism may be to reproduce itself, and it's true that having babies and growing the food to feed them is the life's work of many women and men, but in today's complex society the soul may have a purpose that transcends her individual life. Together, our souls are part of the collective consciousness of humankind. A self-aware soul can work to influence that larger consciousness and improve life for everyone.

There is no shortage of missions in our times. Inspired souls evolve our species from one age to the next by raising the consciousness of the collective mind. Sometimes even a symbolic act can be a catalyst for change in other souls. In the right time and place, the tiniest gesture can shake the world.

When Rosa Parks, tired from her day's work, refused to yield a bus seat to a white man, she triggered massive popular support for the struggling civil rights movement. A twenty-six-year-old preacher by the name of Martin Luther King, Jr., heard about the event and helped to organize the bus boycott, and later would have a profound influence on the entire civil rights movement.

Young Marie Curie arrived in Paris from Poland to begin her studies and discoveries when she was thirty years old. Another woman, Mata Hari, the dancer and spy, found her destiny at twenty-seven, when she shed husband and children, changed her name, and began performing onstage. Sojourner Truth, 27, born Isabella Van Wagener, arrived in New York with her two children, took a domestic position, and began dreaming of ways to free those she had left behind. Getting into a new situation was the first step on the road to fame and her own work, a mixture of spirituality and freedom fighting. Frances Perkins was thirty years old when she felt her acorn begin to unfold. After witnessing the tragic Triangle Shirtwaist factory fire, in which women leaped to their deaths to escape the fire because there were no fire escapes, she devoted the rest of her life to designing worker-friendly environments, and to promoting organizations and public policies to help the American working woman and man. Eventually, she became President Roosevelt's Secretary of Labor. And Barbara Jordan was elected to the Texas State Senate when she was thirty years old, becoming the state's first black senator since 1883. Just to mention a few destinies.

To make a difference, we have to know what we have passion for. Often, it is not until our early thirties that we begin to understand. Don't even try to imagine that you are an exception to this. As the sun ripens the fruit on the tree, we are ripened by Saturn, who rules manifestation. Many begin to build careers at this time. Some go back to school, and others finish or drop out. The thirty-something generation will begin to take over now, thank you. The authorities have to prove themselves; you are no longer obedient cannon fodder marching to the common drum. You can hear your own drums starting to roll. You start thinking about your duty to the world. You start listening more deeply.

This lesson may be hard to understand right now, but don't wait to get on with your life until you are done with it all—you'll be forty soon enough. If you open up to change on schedule, between the ages of twenty-seven and thirty-five, you'll ride on the back of old Saturn.

So what, exactly, goes on when Saturn comes back around? Astrologers call it the psychic center of gravity of the soul. Psychic gravity is what we depend on for stability, what we feel we have to prove to the world, what we demand from ourselves, what we seek to preserve at all costs, and what we respect in others. Its shadow is the need that controls us, whose loss threatens or tests us.

Saturn stirs the cauldron of time, the Fates' favorite magic pot, where they brew the future. Into this seething cauldron you must jump; it will boil the flesh from your bones. It is like death, for you go into the unknown, and it is like birth, for from this womb you are reborn.

Let us look at the beginning of this fate cycle in more detail. From the time you are twenty-seven through somewhere in the early thirties, there is often a sense of being in free fall. You begin to feel "weird," disconnected from a setting in which you used to be at home. For some, the feeling is so intense that they actually leave their old life behind—jobs, family, homes. Removing yourself from your normal surroundings helps you put psychic space between your former self and the person you are becoming. The instinct to get away from it all is a strong one. You have to have space to sort things out. This weird feeling directs your attention to the unseen inner workings of the soul.

It is as if we have jumped back into the cauldron to get a "fate makeover." The Fate goddess Verdandi takes the web of our lives and contemplates what to do with it. She is studying it, too, looking to see what might be missing. She turns it over in her hand (reversals again!) to see what's on the other side, what is hidden, what hasn't been displayed yet. She looks for snags and tangles, picks them free, and suddenly a whole new pattern appears.

I asked my friend Terry Sendgraff, pioneer teacher of aerial dance for women in the Bay Area, "What did you do during your Saturn return?"

She went back to school, she told me, and got a divorce. "I was confused," she added. "It wasn't clear what I was doing."

But out of this confusion comes the beat of the new drummer, a new kind of rhythm, a related but different sound. If you refuse Saturn's call, on the other hand, she may give you grief in the form of depression or some other psychic pain.

The early thirties are the heady, life-changing Saturn cycle years. Let's look at the ways in which women have worked through this period in their lives.

My favorite suffragette, Susan B. Anthony, was twenty-eight years old when she went to a public meeting of the Sons of Temperance. When she got up to speak, they would not let her, because she was female. "The sisters were not invited to speak, only to listen and learn," she was told. For her, that was a turning point. Her response was to organize the Women's Temperance Society of New York, and invite all the silenced women to speak freely there. She was thirty-two years old when she attended her first women's rights conference.

Harriet Tubman, the famous black liberator of slaves, escaped from slavery when she was twenty-nine years old. She did it alone and unaided. Once she had freed herself, freedom became her cause. Within one year of her own escape she started liberating her own family, including her aging parents. She was called Moses because she never lost a passenger.

Elizabeth Cady Stanton, the visionary of the suffrage movement and the author of Susan B. Anthony's speeches, had been
excited about justice since childhood. Her father was a lawyer
and he trained her at home. In her late twenties she married
Henry Brewster Stanton, and for their honeymoon, the radical
couple went to London for an anti-slavery convention. Imagine
her surprise when the women had to sit behind white sheets on
the balcony while the men carried on about equal rights for black
men. But behind that white curtain she met Lucretia Mott, a sea-
soned anti-slavery activist. Together they decided to organize the
historic Seneca Falls Women's Rights Convention in 1848. She
wrote the Declaration of Sentiments along the lines of the Declaration of Independence. Mrs. Cady Stanton was then thirty-two
years old.

As I write, a marble statue of Anthony, Stanton, and Mott,
which was commissioned for the Capitol Building in Washington,
D.C., many years ago, has finally been rescued from the basement
to which it had been relegated, and installed in the Rotunda with
all the statues of the fathers of our country at last. These women
were the Three Fates manifest, who have woven the web of liber-
ties of today for women.

The mystic Saint Teresa of Avila was also in the hands of the
Fates when, shortly after she had taken the veil, at the age of thirty-
two, she fell ill and apparently died. She lay without any sign of life
for four days while her friends watched over her—even when a fire
broke out in the convent—and then she simply revived. She was literally resurrected.

The person she had become was so focused in the spirit that she
would levitate against her will. She tied herself to the furniture
because she had this habit of suddenly floating toward the ceiling
when discussing the Holy Spirit. Her mystical experiences were
stunning and profound. She had visions of Jesus and experienced

several visitations from an angel who pierced her heart with a golden javelin, saying the words "Be filled with the love of God."

What is even more remarkable was that her spiritual experiences gave her the power to take action in the world. She eventually became the abbess of her convent and an important figure in the political life of her time. In her case, the remaking of destiny took the form of actual death and resurrection. Most people go through these experiences only symbolically.

Remember, the Fates must fulfill their own primal directive: "All things must pass." That includes the good and the bad and the ugly and the beautiful . . . and the saintly.

When I jumped back into the cauldron at the age of thirty, I was depressed and suicidal. In the words of the song, I was already coming apart at the seams, more than ready to be torn to pieces and put together in a new way.

The sixties had just come to an end. Everyone was still talking about love, but I had no one to love me. My husband was fond of me, but there was no passion. He'd had a mistress in town for years. Then I met a man "accidentally" and fell in love with him. He already was all I wanted to become, my soul's mirror from a distant future. When everybody was dropping out of society, he had jumped in with both feet and was now running three different film companies. He was burning with a passion for making meaningful documentaries.

I was stoned on romance, pot, and music. But my first big lesson was already on its way. How do you turn a lonely suburban housewife in the throes of her first adult love affair into a feminist witch? "No problem," said Verdandi. "First, we break her heart, then we put her together again!"

The means she chose was to throw a real bitch witch at me. Upon meeting Sonia, I immediately recognized that she was in love with the same man as me. But who would have expected that she would hex the bejesus out of me? One day she came by when my lover and I were down at the pond for a swim and left an arrangement of smooth black stones on the wooden steps in the formation of an XX. The stones were chosen with the intent to throw obstacles in our way.

I will never forget the moment I recognized the hex. I had never seen a hex before in my life; my mother was not into hexes. But something in my soul stopped me in my tracks. My angel said loud and clear, "Don't walk over those stones!" I started to repeat this out loud, but my lover had already stepped over them.

He broke up with me three days later. He just kept repeating over and over, "I just can't . . ."

To learn my first witch lesson, I had to experience the power of a jealous woman's spell. Sonia certainly knew how to cast a mean spell. In my boldness, I inspired that I could actually dismantle a hex by picking up each one, spitting on it, and saying, "Back on you tenfold." Big mistake! Never touch a hex with your bare hands. I broke out in what appeared to be terrible itching bites that nobody could identify, all over the right side of my body. I suffered for six weeks until finally the grief over losing my lover and despair at my loveless life drove me to move to Los Angeles.

Memories about magic that I had heard when I was a child in Hungary were beginning to surface. I knew what I needed, but I didn't know where to find it. It was the fate goddess Verdandi who led me to a metaphysical shop in Hollywood run by two Dianic witches, Rheo and Eileen. Luck or destiny? Both! Rheo and Eileen carried more than self-help books—they had powerful spells, already assembled in shoe boxes. When I explained my problem, they gave me a remedy. It was a reversal spell, which I had to perform for nine nights in a row in order to break Sonia's spell. Each night after I had performed the ritual I would dream that Sonia was yelling at me, "Stop!" When the ritual for the ninth night had been completed and the spell was cast into the earth, my "bites" suddenly disappeared. I was free of her hex!

And something else happened as well. In only three months I reclaimed my own magical power. By doing the reversal spell, I had stirred up all my genetic memories. Each night that I did the spell it came easier. By the ninth night the power was coming out of me, and my soul shook herself free. (For more on this spell, see my earlier books *Grandmother of Time* and *Grandmother Moon*.)

As a result of all this, I made my move to California permanent. I attended my first women's liberation march that August and found the other part of my mission. I have been part of the movement for women's rights ever since. My own herstorical contribution was to link witchcraft with feminism. It has proven to be a powerful medicine for the collective female consciousness not only in California but for women all over the world.

At the age of thirty-one I had become a new woman. This is when I took the name Z. Budapest, in memory of my origins and my birthplace, and in honor of my new self. With the new name my new destiny had begun.

Twenty-five years later I called that man to see how the Fates had treated him. A few weeks after I left he met a woman, whom he married. They remained happily married until her death, which occurred only weeks before my call. The soul is connected to loved ones; time is nothing to the soul. I must have felt his grief. I still feel love for him. Connectedness is not a choice. It is like the weather— it just *is*.

There is a little death that occurs during this time of our lives. It's not easy to say good-bye to Urdh and all her magical play. Our childhood and our youth will mature into the focused power of the adult, but now we have to let go. Whether you look at antiquity or the present, the Fates have a date with us at this conjunction, when the great Saturn returns to home base in your birth chart.

Some of you will feel it at twenty-six or twenty-seven, while others won't sense the shift until they are thirty-five. Do a little soulwork, say good-bye to Urdh, and summon the good Fate Verdandi.

SOULWORK: GETTING FRIENDLY WITH SATURN

When you feel Saturn's influence growing, you may want to get into harmony with it by making (or redecorating) your altar. In cabalistic tradition, the planet Saturn belongs to the sphere of Binah, who is called the Supernal Mother. Her symbol is the cauldron of rebirth. Her color is the black of deep space, womb of the universe. You can cover your altar with a piece of black velveteen, or a black cloth sprinkled with stars.

With silver fabric paint, draw the astrological symbol for Saturn. Add a picture of Saturn, perhaps copied from a natural history magazine or an astronomy text. Get a picture of ancient mother Binah stirring her cauldron, or place a nice bowl on the altar and fill it with fresh water each Saturn's day. If you want to burn incense, it should be myrrh.

Sit down in front of your Saturn altar at night when it is quiet. Light fate-colored candles: black, red, white. Offer three red apples on your altar as a sacrifice. Relax, focusing attention on your breathing, until your mind is still. Then say:

> Ancient Mother, once more I come to you,
> to your womb, your cauldron, your well.
> Receive me, restore me, rebirth me!
> Let me hear your wisdom, learn your lessons,
> understand and fulfill my destiny. . . .
> So mote it be!

Set the bowl of water in your lap and look into it, sitting so that the surface is in your shadow. Breathe in and out slowly and close your eyes. Let your mind drift, and take note of the images that appear. At first your thoughts may be superficial and chaotic. Let them go one by one until your mind is still. The images that come to you then will be like waking dreams. Take note of them. Jot them down in your spirit journal. This could be the same book you jot your dreams in.

Then thank the Goddess, breathe in and out quickly, and blink to break the trance. Set the water back on your altar and blow out the candles. Write down the insight you have received, and meditate on it until you do this rite again.

Verdandi

CHAPTER FIVE

VERDANDI

Give,
Dearest Goddess,
what's
to be given.
I'll take
what's
to be taken
with both hands,
without
hesitation.

LATVIAN WOMEN'S FOLK POEM
NO. 34185.73

By now I know what I'm doing, yes?

It's Beltane—in the old reckoning, the beginning of summer. The book is going well, the year's business is well under way. On the hills, the green grass of spring is already ripening into summer gold, and my garden is overflowing with flowers.

So far this year my altar to the Fates has gotten a lot of action. But it's time to talk to Verdandi, the middle Fate, now. I light a red candle and kindle the incense. On my altar I've placed a ceramic vase of bright flowers. Surely they will please her!

I stand before my altar and kiss my hand three times, saying the little ancient Wiccan poem: "Everything that is thyne is mine, everything that is mine is thyne . . . Tout Tout throughout and about!" Then I call on Verdandi to show me what is coming into being now, and with a rush of energy that makes the candle flame flare and the smoke swirl wildly, she is here!

I'm astonished first to see how very tall she is, towering over me, gesturing with her long fingers, which sparkle with moon rings, silver and gold, set with sapphires and rubies. Bangles jingle on her slender wrists, golden and silver and bronze. The middle Fate goddess is a babe.

She turns toward me.

"Welcome, Spirit of Wisdom!" I greet her.

"I should think so! I want everybody on notice right now!" she exclaims. "I will rule justly and compassionately, unless you cross me! Then I give you grief!"

"Wow! That's coming on pretty strong."

She lifts one queenly eyebrow. "What did you expect? The cuddle club?"

"What happened to your maternal instinct?"

"Grow up! This is not the time for self-pity. You have to get on with your mission in life! I have you for the next thirty years. There is not a moment to waste—so much to do!"

"Yes, ma'am!" I cry. "I'll get back to work right away!"

She raises her other eyebrow, as if wondering why I'm still standing there. Then she whisks away, head high, skirts gathered in both hands, leaving behind her an atmosphere of urgency, efficiency, and common sense that is thicker than the incense in the room.

BECOMING OURSELVES

Verdandi is the middle goddess of the three Norns. She stands tall and queenly, foot tapping as she waits for us to notice her. In a way she is the most important of the three, because she is that which is coming into being. We are shaped by the past and we look forward to the future, but where we actually live is now. Verdandi receives the thread of our lives from Urdh, and as she measures it out, it passes into the keeping of Skuld. The only time we can see it is the present.

In Greek myth, her equivalent is mighty Lachesis, the helper of reincarnating souls. She is the one who gives us our lot in life. How much laughter, how much sorrow, how many good times, how many tears? It's all up to her. Her name means "the Measurer." She is the goddess you have to talk to in prayers about the important issues in life. She measures out the good and the bad. She measures out the materials with which we will fulfill our mission.

Youth and old age frame the middle third of our lives. During Verdandi's reign, our essence unfolds, our gifts mature and are brought forth. This is the prime time of our lives. To our conscious minds she may be new, but to the soul, this Fate goddess is already an old friend. We met before birth when we chose when and where we would incarnate once more, the most important choice of our pre-lives.

Now the implications of that choice are becoming clear, and so she takes charge. Verdandi governs that which is new. If Urdh governed all that we have inherited and been given, to her sister belongs all that we create in this life. Serving her, we become goddesslike, for we are making life. Our creations may be children, relationships, poems, books, scientific breakthroughs, or the best apple pie this side of the great divide. It doesn't matter. Life is a blessed process and this is the best part of it.

Often gatherings linked to events from our past highlight the changes wrought by Verdandi. Recently some friends of mine were reminiscing about college reunions. "I remember my tenth reunion very well," said Diana, who graduated from Mills College in 1964. "I didn't go to the fifth, because I didn't think I had lived up to what was expected of a Mills girl, but by the time the tenth rolled around, I was thirty-one, much more willing to accept who I really was and not worry about what people thought of me."

Aha, I thought, she was moving away from Urdh!

"And what was it like?" I asked her.

"Well, of course, part of the deal at these things is to check each other out, see who looks older or younger than you do, and so forth. I was curious to see if the women I went to school with had changed."

I looked expectant.

"The funny thing was that they hadn't—or not exactly. Maybe it was because they had lost their puppy fat, so you could see the basic bone structure of their faces more clearly, but what struck me at that party was that everyone looked more like themselves."

Reunited with Verdandi's energies, we have to surrender ourselves into her hands and stop hanging on to the past. We all fight her at first, then, realizing it's no use resisting, we accept the changes she brings. Hopefully, we grow up. At some point during her reign we fulfill our potential. There is a magic moment when everything comes into focus, and we know who we are and why we are here. It is an ecstatic feeling. If Verdandi herself is the act of "becoming," then the task she sets us is to become the individuals we really are.

If we learn nothing else, at this point in our lives we learn to give. To give is to summon abundance. We give and we receive. Love flows out from us to others in a multitude of streams as attention, caring, cultivating, irritation, anger—even hatred sometimes flows from love. In Verdandi's school of hard knocks we must learn the nuances, the small details of loving.

Verdandi unwinds the thread of life and weaves it into the tapestry. She holds the famous cornucopia, the magical horn of plenty from which laughter and tears, children and works of art, and lovers pour out with the apples and grapes and grain. She presides over feasts and hard times, oppression and struggle and triumph. Above all, she rules our inner transformations and reveals their connections to the changes that take place in the outer world. It is written. It is woven. It is spoken. Blessed be.

In Norse myth, we are told that the three Norns dip up water from the Well of Wyrd and pour it over the roots of the World Tree (the tree is the self). This unique task is especially Verdandi's job. She doesn't care about the past—she is interested in making things happen right now. She adores playing with creative people. If they will listen to her music, they may find themselves overflowing with ideas.

How can you tell when Verdandi is calling? You think you are all set with your life, you have a family and a good job, yet suddenly you wish you could just get up and go. You are too young, you say, to be tied down. "Who said that?" you wonder. It was Fate. You may think you were content and happy, but Verdandi doesn't care. She has taken over, and your childhood and youthful achievements are history.

The first Saturn return is her spindle. If you are married, she may get you divorced. If you are not married, she may settle you down or remarry you. If you are content, she will discontent you. If you've been discontented for a long time, now she'll give you peace. Whatever Urdh has done, Verdandi will undo. Even those factors that are not reversed will be changed in some way. Of course, people live at different paces. Verdandi can wait. As soon as your guard is down, the soul will wake up, and you're on your way. Verdandi takes hold.

When Verdandi gets a grip on you, she dunks you back into the cauldron. This is the psychic makeover: She steeps you in the stuff of the universe, cooks you in grief or joy or some other emotion until you get strong. Then she pulls you out, shakes you off, and drops you back into the world with a new set of destinies, a different set of desires. People turn around and go through changes that seem overwhelming because they are so unexpected. There will be many more changes, of course, but this is the first cosmic earthquake, the most dramatic. Some people call this time the "midlife crisis," but instead of seeing it as a crisis, I think it is wiser to see it as an important fate date. The restlessness, the conflicting desires, even ill health if it happens, will clear up in time. Everything that wants to happen now is fateful. Don't be afraid to say yes to it. For example, if there is physical pain, explore it. Find out what the pain is telling you about your body and your lifestyle. The pain itself may lead you to your destiny. Many people who go through a physical crisis at this age become healers.

Verdandi rules our second major cycle, from ages thirty to fifty-eight, a prime time for fate-full action. It is now that a woman is at her physical peak, and her energy, her sexual power and passion can make a mark on the world. If she chooses a high goal to devote herself to, she will make a difference. But what do I mean by making a mark on the world? Your very truth changes the world. This is the time to choose a mission.

A woman with a mission can assist the Fates in carrying out their work to transform the bigger picture. The Fates need us to "staff" or to be present in their historical times. It is women who carry the fate of humanity. Whatever women do, the world will soon follow. Whatever happens to women will happen to the world. Now is the time of our lives when the Fates expect us to become conscious to service, surrender to our own higher impulses, invest our time and energy in work of historic significance as well as in looking after our own precious personal lives.

A tall order? Not for the unfolding female principle of the universe. In our times, the female principle is returning as a divine archetype, and nothing can stop her. She is a phenomenon, and she manifests through every one of her daughters. Through the last two thousand years, we have witnessed the complete denial of female power. It has been hidden, or as legend puts it, the Goddess went to sleep. Women's consciousness went underground with her. But now things are changing.

The Goddess is returning. She is awake, she's had her first cup of coffee, and she has gotten a job. She is back in women's art, dreams, and stories. The Goddess spirituality movement is the fastest-growing religion of our times. It goes across race, language, and culture. It is above politics and even gender, not only attracting powerful women, but also the men who love them. It is a shared psychic awareness of the divine female origins of life.

When you live in Verdandi's time, being is becoming—not only allowing it to happen, but choosing which future it is going to be. The beauty of conscious fate workings is that they endure opposition, overcome it, and then set the tone for the future.

Maturity means taking control of our lives. Women were meant to work with the Fates, not to be slaves to them. The Fates delight in acting in partnership with women in the creation of life. So much is under the Fates' control, but women can freely claim their share of power. Whether or not we give birth to children, when we cross into the realm of the second Fate, we must take the role of mother and give birth to our new selves.

In the early seventies, when my friends and I were in our thirties, we had chants to celebrate our rebirthing as we watched one another unfold from our younger selves. Not everyone makes a ritual of it, but this rebirthing is a continuous process during people's third decade.

In our thirties, many of us form new families. Often such families come together at the workplace, where the same group of people may work together for many years. They learn the details of one another's lives, celebrate birthdays, and take care of one another. Others find alternatives to traditional living arrangements. For most of human history, a "family" has consisted of a household that included people of several generations—grandparents, cousins, and aunts—even hired men and helpers. We can think of the extended network of relationships we have built up as our own families at this time.

Verdandi leads us through the second part of our lives. She hands us challenges and puts us through changes, knowing that now, when our energies are at their peak, we can take all she has to give. Take a picture of yourself now and save it. You are looking in the face of Verdandi.

WORKING: WELCOMING VERDANDI

WHEN: A birthday during your Saturn return, or a day when you feel Verdandi's power.

PLACE: Indoors or out.

ACTION: If you are indoors, light black, red, and white candles. When you light a candle, your spirit comes out and listens. Indoors or out, light incense, and let the smoke mingle with the moving air. Speak these words over the smoke as it is rising:

> *Here you come, mighty Verdandi!*
> *Oh, great weaver, mother of many nations,*
> *giver of many destinies.*
> *Be gentle with me as you work my soul into your pattern.*
> *Spin my energy strongly on your spindle.*
> *Spin me health, wealth, and wisdom*
> *on your eternal loom.*
> *Hold the troubles down to just a small trickle,*
> *bring love to my heart's center.*
> *Urdh! Verdandi! Skuld!*
> *Urdh! Verdandi Skuld!*
> *Urdh! Verdandi! Skuld!*
> *I honor your awesome power!*

(Always repeat a phrase three times to seal the spell.)

A VISION QUEST

Here is another way to get intimate with your Fates.

Camping can be easily transformed into a vision quest. Most state and national parks have camping areas. If you know of an area that is fairly remote, and go there in the spring or fall, in the middle of the week, you should have a fair amount of privacy. Choose a campsite as far from the entrance to the grounds, and as far away from other campers, as you can. If you are up to it physically, go to a site where you can go with your backpack, making sure there is water available.

Travel light—a single-person dome tent and a sleeping bag, trail rations and a water bottle, and toilet paper if you are in the wilderness. For ritual gear, a rattle or small drum will be all you need. Learn about the area you will be camping in beforehand, and find out whether there are any poisonous plants or animals you should watch out for. In case of rain, don't forget to take a poncho; make sure your tent has a rain fly, and pitch the tent where water will run off. Physical discomfort can be very distracting from magical experiences. Common sense is a religious duty.

At dusk, when the sun is setting and the night spirits change places with the spirits of the day, make a sacred fire. If you are not an experienced camper, you may want to practice fire building ahead of time. Be sure you have kindling as well as larger pieces that will burn longer, and be sure to build your fire in a fireproof area.

Lay down the kindling and smaller pieces, then take four larger pieces of wood and bless them one by one, holding each in turn up to the sky with your right hand, and saying:

"This wood I bless and dedicate to the east. May the energy and blessings of the radiant dawning enter this sacred fire.

"This wood I bless and dedicate to the south. May the passion and desire of the noontide come into this sacred fire.

"I bless this wood and dedicate it to the west. May the soothing life-giving energies of the setting sun come into my sacred fire.

"I bless this wood and dedicate it to the north. May the sustaining powers of the sleeping sun come into my sacred fire."

Light the fire with a blessing:

> *Laima! Laima! Laima!*
> *Dearest Goddess of the sun!*
> *Kindle this sacred fire,*
> *bless the one who prays to you,*

let your light attract the Fates
in their aspect as the three Graces!

When the fire is going well, sprinkle it with aromatic herbs, such as bay leaves, oregano, or sage: Bring the bundle of herbs with you from home—perhaps even carry it for a time as a talisman.

As the herbs burn, tell the fire about your feelings about this shift in your destiny. See what comes out of your mouth. You will be surprised. When your soul is allowed to speak spontaneously, a poet is born. Talk until your heart feels lighter.

Then throw some cinnamon sticks on the fire for good luck. The spirits love it. You can say something like this:

> *I send you happy energies from Earth,*
> *good-luck sticks of cinnamon!*
> *Send me rays of insight, good opportunities,*
> *and the good luck to accept them. Blessed be!*

You don't have to ask for specific things, because at this point we don't know what our destiny is going to be. I have always known I would be a writer, but I never dreamed that I would start a lasting spiritual women's tradition. The Fates had more imagination, and they had the script. All we need to do is relax, invite the Fates in, and let destiny unfold. In fate work we are trained to tolerate ambiguity. We don't need to know everything ahead of time. This is hard. One wants to be safe.

Watch over your fire until it burns down. As the wood turns to coals, you may see patterns there. Let your mind drift. Be open to what the fire has to say. Then crawl into your sleeping bag, making sure that your fire is completely out. Place a notebook and flashlight next to your bed, and tell yourself that you are going to have a dream of power. Since the ground is hard, you will probably sleep lightly, which will make it easier to wake up still remembering your dreams. Write down whatever you can remember.

If you can, stay in your campsite for three days, eating lightly and speaking to no one. Go hiking, or find a spot with a good view and sit in contemplation. Always keep your notebook handy, and write down the insights that come to you—don't worry about editing your thoughts; every feeling is important. At night you can repeat the fire ritual. If there is a moon, pray to her as well for the sensitivity to move with the waxing and waning of destiny.

At first you may find it hard to concentrate. The busy mind will try to distract you with hopes and fears and anxieties about your job or family. Don't fight these thoughts—just recognize them and let them go. You may find it useful to visualize a flowing river that will float them away. Gradually, as time passes, your mind will become quieter. If you are quiet enough, Verdandi's voice will become clear.

Once the fog clears and your mind is open, your new mission will reveal itself. I give thanks to my Fates that I was fortunate enough to hear when Verdandi spoke to me. Always follow your heart. Pay attention to your passion—like a lamp, passion lights the path the Dearest Goddess wants you to take.

WORKS IN PROGRESS

Our Verdandi years are the time when we "grab the bull by the horns," answer the knock of destiny, hold her hand and even direct it. A friend of mine told me about her transformation. She worked in corporate America till she was forty, when "I had a spiritual upheaval," she said.

"Right on the dime!" I said. "That is the age of spiritual awakening. So what did you do about it?"

One day she went to a herbology conference and met other women on a spiritual path. She experienced the power that can be raised by a circle of women calling on the Goddess together. This awakening changed the entire course of her life. She dropped out of the corporate world and started organizing Goddess events. Now she produces an annual festival for hundreds of women.

Summoning the Fates in Verdandi means hard work and being productive. You are accumulating merit for yourself by righteously devoting all your energy to cause or career. Be aware, however, that you may not immediately realize if your goals start to change. After a while the mission may occupy so much of your life that there is no room for you. You have to remember that you are an eternal soul that will survive all missions, and you have to value yourself. This is not an easy task. But this is the time to discover how. Sometimes it takes a while to catch on. A whole decade can go by before you realize that you are not happy with what you are doing, or have a strong desire to change again, or just simply want to stop for a while, all frantic work.

To learn the lessons of your Verdandi cycle, you have almost thirty wonderful, powerful years. This is a major period for maturation as you get older not only physically but emotionally and spiritually. Your divine "angel" cannot be neglected. While dealing with the world, you also have to acknowledge the spirit. Only then do you get your queen's crown.

When you are in your Verdandi cycle, getting burned out is a real danger. Women must practice relaxation throughout the day and be conscious of the energy they expend being queens. Sometimes less is more. A good queen delegates. A happy queen smells the roses. Investigate herbal recipes for calming, such as chamomile tea. If you combine the herbs with an exercise program, regular meditation, and a well-balanced diet and vitamin regimen, you can calm yourself naturally. Your body is still young enough to serve you, though it will not endure the kind of abuse you could get away with in your twenties. Be kind to your body, but work the spirit hard. Take up a spiritual discipline. Practice yoga or tai chi, which work the body and spirit together. Practice your favorite goddess spells, the ones that especially make you feel empowered.

In queenhood we think we are immortal. We still feel so much energy that we tend to take our bodies for granted. We skip lunch; we skip dinner and diet too much. Because we think we are omnipotent, we may not be focusing on our need for relaxation and inner reflection as much as we should. Do not starve your soul.

Over time, however, this feeling of total control begins to fade. We begin to think about our mortality and what it is we are really trying to prove. We may also hear the ticking of the biological clock—even women who have already had families find themselves looking longingly at babies in the spring. If you have not had children, this is the point at which you will be seriously reconsidering that decision, or desperately trying to get pregnant. As long as you are fertile, you are fair game for the Fates, who can only bring more souls into the world with the help of women.

THE ARCHETYPE OF THE QUEEN

When I use the word *queen,* I am not thinking of some kind of feudal hierarchy. This word has to be reclaimed because it denotes the phase in a woman's life when she is a fully grown, conscious being, secure in her integrity. She is in possession of herself, slave to no one and nothing, ruler of her destiny. This fullness of maturity comes to us in stages, nourished by the challenges we meet. It comes to us as a result of life's adventures.

Mythologically, women in their forties and fifties are manifesting the Goddess in her queen aspect. She is Hera, leader of civilizations and protector of cities. She is Minerva, the goddess of universities and libraries. She is Athena, the inventor and scientist. She is Pomona, goddess of orchards and fruits, and Ceres, the lady of the grain. She is the Madonna as queen of heaven—mother, protector, miracle maker, healer.

She is also Inanna, ruling her city with her studly young lover, Dumuzi, by her side. In the late thirties and forties, a woman reaches the peak of her sexual energy. Even though our desire may seem overwhelming at times, by our third and fourth decades we tend to be secure with our sexuality and can enjoy it without letting it rule us. We appreciate the opportunity to be beautiful and radiate our sexual experience and energy. Fortunately we can be distracted from sexual obsession by another passion—the delight of exercising mature power as queens. The queen is the ruler of law and order. She presides over festivals, gives bread to the people. Her role is the gift of the years. During our Verdandi years we claim meaningful work in the world for ourselves. Sometimes we get it, sometimes we don't, but we haven't lost the desire to command. Love and use your power.

To see yourself in this new role, you may need to make some changes in your self-image. Instead of approaching an unfamiliar situation with the thought "Oh, I've never done this before, I don't know anything," find your "queendom." It could be at home, or in your workplace or community. The knowledge and experience you've acquired from years of coping with all the things a woman is expected to do simultaneously—while making it look easy—have prepared you to deal with anything.

And then move beyond it. Ask yourself, "Is this where I am called to excel?" You may find that everything you have done so far (except for coping) is irrelevant to your interests now. Alice really doesn't live here anymore.

The next few years are for experimentation and risk taking. The cause you find in Verdandi is not the mission that ends all missions. You will go through many other fateful dates when your life will be turned around. This one is almost like a final vacation. You are still young and vigorous enough to put out a lot of energy. Enjoy it, and keep your psychic feelers sharp and tuned in.

The queen often is not appreciated in the patriarchal world. Look at Barbra Streisand. She has been a magnificent queen of her craft for many years, but her power, magnetism, and excellence are resented in Hollywood. While male actors are applauded for their multifaceted talent, such as when they direct and produce their own films, our queen Barbra is often criticized for being "too pushy, too bitchy, too emotional." But she is just right!

People tend to say this about a lot of women who are exceptional. Hillary Clinton comes to mind. If this criticism is applied to you, wear it like a badge of honor. The next time somebody tries to trash you by calling you a bitch, just say, "Thank you so much, I try!" and see the surprise on their face.

As the daughters of the feminist movement mature, women as souls and minds will triumph because what we have achieved will be more important to the collective soul than the sex of the achiever. The archetypal queen is eager to learn and determined to get her points across. She is not only an executive in a workplace, or a superstar, she is an acting, living goddess advancing the evolution of her species.

For the queen, all those qualities that are so often resented—leadership, stridency, pushiness, relentlessness, perfectionism—are necessary. The queen may be running a large enterprise with many people working for her. She will need to be forceful, maintain high standards, and be compassionate at the same time. She will be required to use her whole mind and all her power at last.

Fate Dates on the Road to Queenhood

At thirty-three, you step on the first big land mine on Verdandi's road of life. You thought all was just going along as planned, and "out of the blue" something has happened. More often than not, the event is something dramatic and life changing. Uranus has moved into opposition to your natal position. Uranus is the planet of change, one of the transpersonal wheels of life in the hands of the Fates. When it opposes us a few times in our lives, we really feel its impact.

In my own life, I was arrested for fortune-telling at thirty-four, tried and convicted as a witch at thirty-five. This threw my entire life into another gear. I had suddenly become famous, gone from being the barefoot pagan priestess on the Malibu mountain to a crusader for the Goddess—teaching in my candle shop, giving speeches at universities, giving workshops on the beach, and traveling around the country promoting the sacred. For the first time in my life a private passion for witchcraft gained political importance and became the healing tool that women could once again use to help themselves spiritually. I was elated at my new role and took to it with relish. My life has never been the same. This service of reviving women's mysteries turned out to be my contribution to women's liberation.

A friend of mine, a young medical doctor from Vienna, refused to go into practice after she received her degree at the age of thirty-three, because she had a huge inner conflict. "I don't know what sickness is!" she cried passionately. "I don't know what healing is! I cannot work on people! My schooling taught me nothing!"

She decided to move to California and enroll at the Taoist Center for Healing in Oakland, where she learned the ancient healing techniques of Chinese medicine and gained perspective on what sickness and healing are all about. Later she figured out how to combine Eastern and Western medicine and now has a flowering practice in her native Austria.

We complete the first quarter of the second Saturn cycle around the age of thirty-seven to thirty-eight, although as with all the other fate dates, it may take a couple of years for the effect to make itself known. The task at this point in our lives is to question authority, to shed the tyranny of the anonymous "they" who we've been worrying about for so long.

The soul-searching we do at this point requires us to reconsider the "old value systems" we acquired at age twenty-nine or thirty. Why so soon? We've just gotten on track and now we're already being asked to question them? Think of it as a recalibration. We are seeking our true identity; if we have begun to develop a persona that doesn't come from the authentic center of the soul, better to discover it now, before we get stuck in it.

It was during this period of my life that I began to let go of my "hippie" lifestyle. This was a very difficult change for me to make. I loved being a flower child—I dressed the part in miniskirts, loved loud rock-and-roll music, and lived to dance. Simply hanging out with my friends was enough of a purpose in life for me. I made enough money to live on working as a gardener, and daydreamed about getting a little storefront and opening a candle shop. I was already doing the work that was my destiny, but I didn't realize it.

My spirituality was a backdrop to my life, not its center. It came to the forefront every six weeks at the Wiccan Sabbats, which were more than just local celebrations because many women came from far away to experience them. Being a priestess came naturally; my soul had been trained to do this through many earlier incarnations. I had imagined destiny as being more work and less fun. Looking back, I realize that our destined path is often less work and more fun than we might think at first. Whatever is flowing "effortlessly" is what we were meant to do.

As we become aware of our destiny, we often undergo a major shift in attitude. If we are lucky, we are still able to respect our old mentors as colleagues.

By the time you reach your next Saturn checkpoint, the path of your Verdandi destiny will have been revealed to you. Sometimes, as happened to me when I became a full-time priestess, it is something that was yours all along. It was in your face, maybe even too close—a hobby, perhaps, an avocation that turns out to be your vocation after all.

Once you gain a little distance from your past you can put it into perspective. Be realistic but not severe. Don't berate yourself if you haven't gotten as far as you wanted to. You are not even halfway into your second destiny! In your thirties and forties you can accomplish a great deal. Apply yourself to whatever is visible and feasible. Don't hesitate to take on challenges—don't wait around; the time for any kind of waiting is over!

The good Fate Verdandi gets us thinking about our lives; she likes to turn the weave over to the other side. She puts questions into your mind: "What if I walk away from all this?" "What if I just stopped going to the office and lived somewhere else?" "What if I leave this relationship, change totally, have a makeover, lose weight, become somebody else?" "Is this all there is?" In Verdandi this kind of thinking is normal. She is a destiny that likes to turn people around, look at the other side of them, and figure out how to make them bloom.

The Fates' directive for these years is to destroy false identities. You need to answer the questions: What assumptions did I make about family values, loving, social behavior that were influenced by patriarchal culture? (Well, we know the answer—it is "everything." Analyze.) In your own upbringing, how did this happen? Which specific assumptions were they? Assumptions about yourself, your loved ones? Are these concepts still valid? And is this all there is to your life?

In my case this was the time in my life when I had to ask myself, "Who am I without a group? Who is Zsuzsanna? Who is Z?" I had been serving the Goddess since I was thirty-one, and now at thirty-seven, I was totally identified with the cause. Service to the mission and my own life were one. But was my total devotion really necessary? Or was it all right to have an independent life on my own? Could I have a lover who was not a witch? Could I ever write something that had nothing to do with the Goddess? Could I just put it all down and walk away for a year?

Soulwork had to be done in order to complete this wrenching time, which lasted for more than a year. Don't even think that dismantling your old self will be a short-term job. On top of everything you've gone through already, all the transpersonal planets are going to roll in before you reach forty, as the Fates really work their spinning wheels.

For practicing soulwork at this stage, I recommend a lot of self-loving acts. Get massages, take vacations, get together with others, and do special things for yourself. Read a lot, including books not related to your work. If you had a problem with self-image before, now is when all your old self-loathing tapes will turn on. Don't ignore them—listen and try to understand what they are telling you. Reinterpret them in the light of what you know now, then bless them and let them go. Knowing what's going on astrologically will help you to understand, but it won't make the need for self-examination go away.

On your fortieth birthday use lavender-colored candles, in honor of Neptune. This year is the spiritual awakening if you haven't had one yet. Take up swimming; submerge in water often. Walk on the seashore or a riverbank. Imagination is now highlighted. To get in harmony with Neptune, wear a lot of soft, muted colors, and listen to music as often as possible. Meditate, and if possible, join a women's spiritual group. At this time, writing talents may also surface. If you haven't been keeping a journal, now is a good time to begin one. You have been ripened, you have lived, and now you have something to say. Take a moment to identify your favorite illusions about yourself and the world, and dissolve them in your imagination like sugar cubes in a cup of tea.

The mid-forties are a time when many women pause and take some time to look inward. Whatever makes you sad, oppressed, unhappy, shed it now. Accept the conditions that are present in your life and move on. Allow all your feelings and your pain to surface—let your soul get drenched with the inner tears. The soul may need this downtime to develop further. Turmoil is fertile soil necessary for the soul to find eternal wisdoms, insights, and eventual peace of mind.

This changing may be hard on your nerves, but your heart grows lighter when you move with destiny. Whatever makes you feel more free is the path to follow. Verdandi will pull you along. It's her turn. You are responsible for understanding your own feelings—what you want, and what you will not tolerate anymore. Your new desires are blessed by the Fates.

I know of a woman who, in her early forties, challenged convention by leaving her marriage of many years and running off with her lover, who was from a different cultural background and of a different ethnicity from her. She lived with the new lover for a few years, but when her Saturn opposition came around, she left him and moved on, still seeking authentic intimacy, until she found a lover with whom she settled down for a long-term relationship. Her changes involved a profound sexual awakening. She took risks yet also had the wisdom and confidence to realize when it was time to continue on in her life until she found a partner with whom she had mutual respect. She ended up with a large circle of loved ones, good relationships with both her lover and her children.

Through the ages, women and men have been aware that there are parts of life that aren't fun yet are necessary. It is a difficult leap of faith to suffer and then acknowledge that the suffering was good for us, at least at the time. Later on, this may be much easier. Often we can look back and say, "Well, if I hadn't broken my leg, I never would have met my dearest love" or "Had I won the contest, I never would have been elected to office," etc. Like the story of the little girl who looked at the pile of horse manure and concluded that there must be a pony in there somewhere, with experience you learn to look for ways to make your disasters work for you.

The nature of "service" is self-transformation that is of use to others. It is going to serve the old lady in the fairy tale, picking her apples and taking out her bread, fluffing up her pillows so that snow can fall. The reward for good service is another job. Even a queen receives honor and assistance only so that she can more efficiently serve her people.

What you do at this time of your life affects the planet. You are at the height of your powers; if you direct your will now, you'll go far and have enough time to see your own harvest come in. Some of us get showers of golden coins as a reward, while those who won't serve get tar and feathers. If I may paraphrase the good president John F. Kennedy, this is a time when you ask not what the Fates can do for you but what you can do for the Fates. History is in our hands. Within the great tapestry of planetary destiny there are many patterns into which we can weave our threads. It is far better to work with Verdandi than to be thrust into the web by the Fates without our will. As Jung said, free will means that I cheerfully do what must be.

RITUALS: MORNING ENERGY

What if you don't have the energy to cope with Verdandi's blessings? Here is a procedure for powering up.

The moment when you get up in the morning is a fateful one. In many cultures it is believed that if you get up on the "wrong side" of the bed, you will have bad luck all day long.

But which side of the bed is the "right" side? If you leap out of bed at the first ring of the alarm clock, into clothes laid ready and shoes set pointing toward the door, you are already working, even before you leave home. When you get up this way, without a thought for yourself, you ignore the spirit and miss the opportunity to empower yourself.

If you need an alarm to wake up, choose one with as gentle a ring as possible, and set it fifteen minutes ahead of when you really have to get up. Spend that time on getting your soul ready for the day. Train yourself to hang on to those last moments of semiconsciousness, and use them to remember your dreams. Check in with yourself.

After the first deep sleep of the night, most of us spend the rest of the night in a dream state. Often a dream seems to be a simple processing of current events, though even the boring dreams will tell you something about your real concerns. Sometimes, though, your unconscious will drag up from the depths a dream of deep significance. These dreams may be repeated, with variation. When you have a dream like this—a dream of power—pay attention. Keep a little notebook beside your bed, and before you do anything else, or even think of anything else, write down your dreams.

Take the next few minutes to get in touch with your body. How is it feeling when you're still lying down? How does it feel when you begin to move? Watch a cat as it wakes up—turning and stretching luxuriously before it begins its morning "bath." We are animals, too, and a good stretch brings pleasure. If there's time, "feminate" (a postpatriarchal word for masturbate) to awaken all your senses.

If you are older, or have lower-back trouble (as most of us who spend large portions of our day sitting in front of computers do), begin with some sciatic stretches. Do some abdominal curls, tightening your tummy muscles. Do what feels good—your body will tell you. By this time your circulation should be kicking in, getting you ready for the day—and you are still lying in bed!

When you do get up, warm up your mind with an affirmation: "Today I am the channel for healing energy in the universe," or perhaps, "Today I am the channel for prosperity in the universe."

Now you are ready for that first cup of jasmine tea or green tea and the invigorating shower with lavender-scented soap, and for all the other tasks of the day.

TAKING A SPIRIT BREAK

You take coffee breaks; why not take a break from work to refresh your spirit?

One of the major illusions of modern life is that we are our jobs. It isn't so. We are not our jobs, we are spirits embodied in flesh that perform useful functions in the world. In the Middle Ages, people were born into classes and guilds, and followed their parents into the family trade. They thought they were their "class." Today, not only can we choose our careers, but most of us will have several different careers over the course of our lifetimes.

Jobs can be deadly or fulfilling. As our spirits grow and change, it is not the new job that changes our destiny, but we ourselves who look for work that will serve the needs of the people we are becoming. But even the best job has moments of drudgery that weigh down the spirit. You can renew your enthusiasm for a good job, and your endurance for a bad one, by taking a "spirit break."

When your blood sugar is lowest—say, around three o'clock in the afternoon—put down your work. Set your computer on "sleep" and turn off whatever other machines you may be using. (Even factories are required to give workers break times at regular intervals.) Open a window or go outside where you can get some fresh air.

Begin by breathing deeply, in and out. Pay attention to the flow of air in and out of your lungs. As you inhale, imagine that you are taking in energy from the universe. When you exhale, give your wastes back to the universe to be recycled. As you breathe, remind yourself that each one of us is only a few breaths away from death. Without that life-giving oxygen, you will lose consciousness, and all the processes in your body will cease.

Thinking about death wakes you up to what's important in life. Follow the progress of your breath in and out with reverence— such a small and automatic action that makes so great a difference! Appreciate the fragility of life, and the beauty.

If you have privacy, you can chant the following prayer to the winds; otherwise, say it silently.

I [name] am calling on the winds,
On the winds of change
On the northern wind
called Nemere
the bringer of souls
opener of wombs!
Dearest directions,
send me lucky winds
to blow my body clean with your breath,
and let me walk in health, wealth, and wisdom.
Blessed be!

Now that your blood has been re-oxygenated, have a cup of tea. Use a special cup, one whose shape and texture give you pleasure, not paper or (shudder) Styrofoam. Choose jasmine or rose hip tea. Jasmine is aromatic and energizing—it was used by the ancients to counter depression—and rose hip tea is both nutritional and esoteric. When you drink it, you are drinking in the heart of the rose, a symbol of the beauty, life, and wisdom of the Goddess. By drinking its tea, you infuse your body with its magic and get a good shot of vitamin C as well. This whole process will take about ten minutes, and when you are done, you will feel totally rejuvenated.

PROTECTION RITUAL

One of the most universal human needs is for protection. Naturally, the ability to protect is a basic characteristic of our gods. Most prayers at least mention it. We need to be protected when we are born, as we go through life, even after death. It is often not clear whether we should be asking for protection by the Fates or from them, since they often seem to work at random, giving good and bad times to everyone without exception.

How, then, can we improve our chances to be safer in the cosmic chaos? By doing a ritual to the Fates, we attune our spirits to their workings, and by honoring them, we notify the forces that rule destiny that we are willing to work with them, instead of having to be hit on the side of the head to make us pay attention. Stupid is as stupid charms. We all hunger for truth magic, the chance to be special.

Wait to do this ritual at a time when you feel you can concentrate on a spell. The nights of the full moon are good because the energy of the Goddess is strong then and the Fates draw closer.

Get three fresh eggs, brown or white ones, and dye them red with vinegar and food coloring. Dyed eggs are very traditional offerings (the earliest ones have been found in Dark Age Germanic tombs). Write your name on each one.

Find a cave or hollow in the side of a hill. Dig a hole and bury the eggs in the earth. Then say:

> *Blessed be these eggs as my offering to the Old Ones.*
> *As the Fates are weaving,*
> *as the Fates are spinning,*
> *as the Fates are cutting us loose,*
> *your scissors will spare me,*
> *your curses won't find me,*
> *only your blessings will flow.*
> *Clotho, Lachesis, Atropos,*
> *Urdh, Verdandi, Skuld,*
> *Alecto, Tisiphone, Megaera,*
> *These red eggs are for your pleasure.*
> *And my spell comes true.*

SOUL WALKS

The soul needs to meander about, roam, feel itself moved by the primal forces. Because your soul is in a body, one way to help her feel this is for your body to walk as well—this is also good exercise.

In the morning, or on your lunch hour, or when you get home from work, find a park or someplace wild to go walking. Take three red apples with you, and when you find a spot that draws you, toss the apples out for the local wildlife to receive on behalf of the Fates. Pray:

> Red apples to the Weird sisters I offer,
> Red apples they like to eat.
> Thanks and honor to the Old Ones
> through the ears of the wild things they shall hear.

PRETTY MAID IBRONKA

Whose steeds
of wind
prance
before
the church door?
They belong
to
the Dearest Goddess
in the golden
carriage.
She's come
to take
my sister
away.

LATVIAN WOMEN'S FOLK POEM
NO. 54814.170

This is a fairy tale about a woman coming to grips with her second destiny. There are not too many of these. There are plenty of stories of women in their first destiny, of course, but as soon as the heroine finds her man, the story ends. Usually that's the only way to leave the story with a happy ending. In real life, to "get married and live happily after" used to mean a short ten or twenty years more of life, breeding five kids and dying of exhaustion. Otherwise, women star only in sad ballads (we are victims) or dramatic stories (we die).

This story follows a woman through her struggle with a force much greater than herself. She has one adviser, a wise woman. She is transformed, dies, and is reborn. Her adversary is the demon lover, born from her frustrated desire.

Once there was a beautiful young maiden named Pretty Ibronka, who could not find a sweetheart. She was the prettiest of all the women in her small town, but she felt unattractive, and this was because she was the only girl of age in the village who didn't have a sweetheart. It was humiliating. Nobody knew why this was—she was sweet, modest, healthy, and bright. And she was deserving as well. A hard worker. A desirable catch on all counts.

In her village it was the custom of the young to gather and spin yarn from wool, drawing out the thread like the Fates themselves. All the girls had sweethearts, young men who came to sit with them while they spun their wool and to talk about this and that. One night as Ibronka sat alone, listening to the happy murmur of conversation around her, the pain of her need became so great, it turned into a wish, a fate wish, which comes deep from the heart.

"I wish God would give me a sweetheart, even if he was from the devil," she said. As she spoke the words, she shivered as if she had been brushed by the winds of power, and she knew that what she had uttered in the sacred spinning place would come true.

That very evening a tall young stranger came through the door and sat next to Pretty Ibronka. He wore a long sheepskin coat and a hat with a single egret feather. He was handsome, and better still, he was interested in her.

As the custom was, they began to talk. But Ibronka, remembering her wish, was flustered and she dropped her spindle. As she reached down to pick it up, her fingers brushed the young man's feet, and she could feel that what looked like boots were actually cloven hooves. She looked again to make sure of it but said nothing, because he was very handsome. And as the custom was, when she saw him out at the end of the evening, she gave him an embrace. But as she put her arms around him she felt them go right through his body. Now she was truly alarmed. But still she said nothing to the other girls.

Instead, she sought counsel from an old woman in the village, the wise woman Emese, the local healer.

"Oh, Mother," she pleaded, "what can I do? I was so tired of being the only one in the village without a sweetheart that I wished God would send me one, even if he was of the devil!" And she told her the whole story. "Please put me right, make me wise. Mother, what should I do?"

"Well," Emese said, "you certainly seem to have got what you asked for! Try moving around—change the place you go to spin, see if he follows you."

Ibronka did as she was told, every night sitting to spin in a different place. But every night the tall stranger came and sat next to her to keep her company, so she went back to the old woman again.

"Mother, he's followed me everywhere. I don't know what to do. I didn't dare to ask him about himself, but I know he's no mortal man."

The wise woman's face darkened with worry. She leaned closer to Ibronka and said, "Tie the end of your yarn to his *suba* (sheepskin coat) when the spinning is over and follow him to see what he does. But whatever happens, don't let him know what you saw or he can take your soul to hell. This is very important."

She did as she was told. She tied the yarn to his *suba* and when the evening was over she followed it as it unwound all the way to the churchyard. There she peeked through the keyhole and saw her "sweetheart" sawing a head into halves just like people slice a melon, and feasting on the brains of a dead man. When she saw this she got so horrified she broke the thread and ran back home. But the devil must have seen her, because as soon as she got home and closed the doors behind her, she could hear him call under her window:

"Pretty maid Ibronka, what did you see peeping through the keyhole?"

"It was dark. Nothing did I see!"

"You must tell me what you saw or your sister will die!"

"Nothing did I see. If she dies, we will bury her," she said, and her sweetheart went away.

But the next morning her sister was dead. Ibronka ran to see the old woman again and told her what had happened.

"Mother, my sister is dead. What should I do?"

"Put her body in the shed. Don't bury her," the wise woman advised.

That evening she didn't dare to go out to spin, but stayed home. Nonetheless, her demon sweetheart showed up under her window and called to her:

"Pretty maid Ibronka, what did you see when you looked through the keyhole?"

"Nothing did I see."

"You must tell me what you saw or your mother will die."

"If she dies, we will bury her."

Ibronka went to bed with cold sweat all over her. When she woke up her mother was dead.

She mourned and cried and went to see the old woman.

"Don't worry about it," the old woman said. "Put her corpse in the shed. Don't bury her."

Ibronka did as she was told. The evening came and she knew that her father was next. It wasn't long before she heard her sweetheart outside.

"Pretty maid Ibronka, what did you see when you spied on me through the keyhole?"

"Nothing did I see," she insisted.

"Then your father will die."

"If he dies, we'll bury him," she said defiantly.

Sure enough, the next morning her father lay dead. She put him into the shed as well.

Now I am left alone, she thought.

The old woman said to her, "You know what is going to happen next. You shall die. Now, go to your friends and tell them that when you die they must not take you out in a coffin through the door or through a window."

"Then how?"

"They must cut a hole through the wall and push the coffin through it. And they should not carry you to the churchyard on the usual roads, but use backyards and alleys, and when they get you to the churchyard, they must bury the coffin in a ditch just outside the regular burial grounds."

Ibronka told her friends what she wanted to happen. They gathered around her, not believing that she would die, but then sleep overcame them, and when they woke up, Ibronka was dead, too.

They realized then that all she'd told them was true, so they followed her instructions, carried her out through the hole in the wall, bore her to the churchyard by backyards and alleyways, then buried her in the ditch just outside the graveyard.

On the day she was buried the demon sweetheart turned up under her window. He called her name, but when nobody answered, he grew impatient and kicked in the door. "Tell me, door," he said, "did they carry her through you?"

"No, they didn't," the door answered.

"Tell me, window, was it through you they took her out?"

"No, it wasn't," answered the window.

"Tell me, road, was it on you that they took her away?"

"No, it was not," the road answered.

"Tell me, graveyard, was it here that they buried Ibronka?"

"No, she is not here."

After all these questions he was no more the wiser, and very frustrated.

"I must put on iron boots and take an iron staff and search until I find my Ibronka, even if I have to wear my iron boots to shreds."

And so he went away.

Time went by. A tall, beautiful rose grew from Ibronka's dust. The grave was not far from the road, and one day a prince drove by and saw the beautiful rose. First he sent his coachman to pluck the flower for him, but the flower was stubborn and didn't come off, so the prince himself had to go and get it. Then it came happily.

At home the prince made a special place for the rose in front of a round mirror so he could see it even from his dining room, so ravished was he by its beauty. That night he and his servant ate well, but he left some food behind. When he came back for a snack later on, all the leftovers were gone. At first he thought that his servant had eaten them, but it happened again and again, so he finally asked the coachman if he was finishing off the meals he'd left behind.

The coachman denied it, so the prince decided to watch over the food and see what happened to it. As midnight struck, he saw the rose bend down and become a beautiful maiden. It was Ibronka. She seated herself at the table and feasted on the leftovers. She drank a little water afterward and was about to turn into a rose again when the prince embraced her and said, "My beautiful beloved sweetheart! You are mine and I am yours forever, and nothing but death can part us."

"It cannot be," said Ibronka. "There is more to it than you think!"

But the prince wooed her with so much feeling that at last she gave in, with one condition: "I will marry you if you never compel me to go to church."

The prince didn't understand this, but because he loved her so much, he agreed.

So they were married and were happy. Ibronka had love in her life at last. She bore two children, and it was their father who took them to church. She wouldn't go herself.

Years went by and still Ibronka would not go to church with them. Eventually the community started wondering, for in general it was the wives who were faithful churchgoers, not the husbands. So the priest finally asked the prince about it.

"That is the custom with us," he answered. But he resented Ibronka for embarrassing him, so when he went home he confronted her about the situation.

"Why can't you come? Give me a reason," he said.

"My husband, we have an agreement."

"I am tired of the scorn of the country. I want us to make a new agreement."

"If we do, then you will lose me," she said. "But if you insist, you and I will go to church together."

To church they went, and as the mass came to a close, a ragged man in worn iron boots approached the couple. Out of the prince's earshot he said, "I pledged myself, Ibronka, to put on the iron boots and to take the iron staff and look for you even if I wore the iron to shreds. But just before I wore them out completely, I have found you! Tonight I shall come to you."

Then he went away, leaving Ibronka weeping.

"What did that man say to you?" the prince wanted to know.

"Wait and see and you will learn what will come of making me go to church with you!"

And soon enough after they'd returned home, they heard him calling under the window: "Pretty maid Ibronka, what did you see through the keyhole?"

This time she told the whole story but with a twist. With each and every sentence she would add, "But to a dead man, not a living one, I am speaking," as the wise woman had told her to do long ago.

"I was the prettiest girl in the village—but to a dead man, not a living one, am I speaking—and all the other girls had sweethearts but me. Once I prayed to God to send me a sweetheart even if he was of the devil. There must have been some special way I said it— but to a dead man, not a living one, I am speaking—because that evening a young man appeared dressed in a *suba* and a hat with a single egret feather. He greeted us and took his place next to me—but to a dead man, not a living one, am I speaking . . ."

All this time she was telling her story the devil underneath her window bellowed and threatened, yelling louder and louder: "Pretty maid Ibronka, what did you see spying on me through the keyhole?"

But Ibronka had been through a lot and she was going to finish this, and so she went on, repeating with every phrase that it was to a dead man, not a living one, that she was speaking.

"There was an old woman in the village. I asked her for advice, and she put me wise, but to a dead man, not a living one, am I speaking . . ."

Each time she said this last line, the devil suffered greatly and demanded more and more persistently that she answer him. But still she continued her tale.

"And my friends cut a hole through the wall, and carried my body by backyards and alleyways and buried me in a ditch. But to a dead man, not a living one, am I speaking."

Then the demon lover collapsed under her window. He uttered a shout that shook their castle to its foundations, and then it was he who died.

At that moment, Ibronka's mother and father and sister rose from their long, enchanted sleep in the shed and came back to life. They walked outside and joined the rest of the folks. The wise woman was there with blankets and jugs of water.

And that was the end of it.

What the story implies is that Ibronka's second destiny will be unclouded and that her life will continue without fear until she dies a normal death. What about her relationship with her prince? Does this come between them? The story doesn't say, but one can hope that their troubles are over with.

This woman from folk tradition is not so different from many modern women. As a girl she is so desperate for love and the status it brings that she gets involved with a devil. She is pushed to the end of her strength, and finally into death itself, in order to escape this supernatural tormentor. Her death is the only way out of this first painful destiny.

But her death, like many experiences in which a person's life is destroyed, is a positive transformation. She becomes a rose, symbol of the Goddess, and enters into a new fairy existence in which by day she lives as a flower and at night comes back as a woman and eats food. This is her second incarnation. She is resurrected by love.

A prince, the masculine power in its positive aspect, falls in love with her, takes her home, transforms her from maiden to mother. This is her third destiny, and she is happy there. Now she has to fight for it. Pay the dues. Settle the score with the devil. It is significant that the devil visits in the house of God, the Church. In this fairy tale the devil is a Christian god. By the time the demon lover rediscovers her in the church, she has long left behind the destiny that still binds him.

Only now is she mature enough to tell her truth and destroy the devil.

In Hungarian fairy tales the poor devil always gets the short end of the stick, no matter how powerful he seems to be. Especially women, especially grandmothers, outwit him regularly.

Ibronka's transformation into a rose is a kind of qualitative quantum leap of consciousness. From a dumb, hungry girl, she becomes part of nature, part of beauty. Many of us do that as a mission. We don't bury our dead; they're just waiting in the shed for when we are ready and strong enough to confront our past. Ibronka matured and was forgiven.

CHAPTER SIX

CHIRON AND THE SECOND SATURN RETURN

If you wish
earnestly
for dignity,
the Dearest Goddess
will bring you
a wreath
of flowers.
If you don't
reach for it,
all you
may get
is a wreath
of thistles.

LATVIAN WOMEN'S FOLK POEM NO. 39406.3

The invitation came in a cream-colored envelope, the kind people use for wedding announcements or graduation invitations. But it was September, not June, and I couldn't think of anyone I knew who was getting married. Still, it certainly looked more interesting than the bills and the junk mail, so I dropped the rest of the mail back on the table and opened it.

Laurie Margaret's daughter invites you to a party to celebrate her fifty-eighth birthday and Ops return. . . .

For a minute I just stared at it. Then I started to laugh.

In Roman mythology, the wife of Saturn is Ops, the goddess whose name gives us the word *opulence*. She is the lady with the money! And Laurie is one of the most optimistic people I know.

Leave it to Laurie to put a positive spin on her second Saturn Return by renaming it for the goddess of plenty!

The party was as memorable as the invitation. There was a lot of really wonderful food and drink, and every woman over the age of fifty-eight who attended got to wear a golden party crown.

VERDANDI'S CROWN

To understand the second Saturn return, we need to look at it in the context of the first one, which occurs between the ages of twenty-eight and thirty. This was the first time we realized we were no longer children and that the purpose of our lives needed to be discovered. Human beings are the slowest animals to mature. Most mammals are on their way with their lives when we are just waking up psychically. But that is the big difference between us and the rest of the living animal world: They are on perfect automatic and we are on cyclical manual. We may breed and feel by the moon, but we grow up by Saturn.

Our souls demand their purpose. It is almost as if we are housing an important space traveler, who is inhabiting our animal bodies for as long as it takes to accomplish a spiritual goal. The traveler is not always kind to the dearest body. They are united yet often they have conflicting demands. Today, for example, the writer in me says that I must spend my prime energy working on this book, whereas my body would like to take a walk on the beach and pick up shells from the sand. But the writer is at the controls and will win out.

As the grande dame planet Saturn (or Ops!) moves slowly toward the next thirty years of our lives, a new destiny is brewing. This destiny is the gift of Skuld. The Lady of That Which Must Be will give us thirty more years in which to complete our work and, what is more important, to understand and *appreciate* our purpose in being here. Some of us will complete this task sooner and move on; others may stick around for yet a fourth Saturn return in which to put a final polish on our souls.

You may find that your dream life is more active now. Mystical, magical things start happening to you more visibly. You notice inner events better. Your ability to be introspective is growing. Meditate every day, and start keeping a personal journal if you have not yet done so. Write down your feelings every day.

CHIRON: THE WOUNDED HEALER

The changeover to the second Saturn return develops out of the Chiron return, which occurs between the ages of fifty-one and fifty-two and often brings a shamanic healing crisis. In mythology, Chiron is the wounded healer and teacher, the most effective kind. In astronomy, Chiron is a comet with a highly elliptical orbit around the sun, a visitor from another galaxy that wanders over to ours regularly. Mythology tells us that Chiron can travel between different worlds or realities and bring knowledge to us. The shamanic transformation we experience as a result of the Chiron return requires a crisis—either a physical wound or an emotional one.

In my own life it was a physical trauma. I was in a car "accident" at the age of fifty-one. It was a slow-speed accident, and the other car was driven by a woman named Rose, who was my age and, like me, had never been involved in any traffic accidents before now. It smelled like the work of the Fate goddess all the way. Chiron in one accident. Nobody was hurt seriously. Or so it seemed.

But what happened? The doctors didn't notice that my hips were twisted slightly and that my fibula was rotated out. This unattended dislocation didn't really make itself apparent until two years later, when my body shut down in pain. To find the right doctor took another two years. By the time I found effective help, I had arthritis in both hips and knees, plus a touch of osteoporosis. I started feeling the touch of the old woman, the finger of fate. When I finally learned the stretches that helped my bones to align each morning, things began to improve, and after a few years I could finally live without painkillers again. When I emerged from this crisis, I was already into my "crone phase," and grateful for having survived to reach it.

I used to say, "The death goddess kicked me—I was so strong before." But looking at my body in detail for the first time uncovered an additional long-term problem with my lower back. I spent most of my fifties learning how to maintain my health, involved in meticulous exercises, developing self-discipline. Croning is not for cowards.

For most of us, though, it is menopause that can create the Chiron health crisis, a journey into the world of self-healing. You learn how powerful small things are, like hormones and calcium. You can carry evening primrose around so you can take it when power surges hit, like sudden sweats. Learning some form of healing and dealing with health problems left over from earlier years is part of the regenerational work of the Fate goddess that we are forced to accept, usually by experiencing pain.

The spiritual task of this cycle is to confront any core, unhealed wounds, either psychic or physical, mental or spiritual, that keep us from fully integrating body and soul—to confront them, then to dismember and remember. In shamanic terms, you have to die a little in order to be reborn. Shamans are said to "fall" into trance and appear dead, sometimes for weeks. People know not to move them from where they fell, nor to disturb them in any other way. In Hungary in the old days they would merely put a blanket over the person, even if it was winter, and leave him there until he regained consciousness.

In traditional societies, when those who have been through a shamanic trance revive, they teach others what they learned in the otherworld, what the gods taught them. These teachings may be about healing—what to use to heal what ailments. Or the shaman may bring back information about weather patterns (why there is a drought, for example, and a spell to make rain).

In our own lives the Chiron crisis gives us an opportunity to confront old patterns of abuse and self-destructiveness. It can act as a catalyst to send us on a do-or-die search for healing. And often you discover that you have what it takes. Our bodies do know how to repair themselves. When you are pushed to the wall, you find that you have the healing powers yourself, and you can get well again. The best part is when you become the wounded healer yourself, helping others who are less fortunate than yourself.

Emotionally you may start feeling this shift around age forty-nine; as you approach the Chiron shift, you slowly learn how to switch from feeling wounded yourself to healing the wounds of others.

By the time you reach your second Saturn return (at age fifty-eight), most likely you will have completed the physical transitions of menopause, though you are probably still struggling with the spiritual implications. The average age of menopause is around fifty, which means that in general a woman's physiology is beginning to settle down before she has to deal with the deeper spiritual changes of the Saturn return. Just as the first menstruation signals the beginning of adolescence, menopause is the beginning of a decade of transformation into a crone.

Use herbal remedies such as evening primrose or dandelion root to alleviate the hot flashes. Consult a good doctor about your health. You are no longer immortal—that biggest of illusions is finally revealed. Dissolve it. Find your own tonic in nature by learning about health and how to prevent problems, and take it daily.

Even if you've never paid attention to your body, you will have to do so now. Your metabolism, your sex drive, your energy level—all of these are changing as your hormone mix readjusts itself. As the estrogen/androgen ratio changes, a woman may find herself becoming more forceful and self-confident (men, on the other hand, whose androgen levels are falling, often mellow out). You do yoga, you exercise, you walk and swim. You change your diet, you take pills for this or that. You start reading up on materials about health and learn more about your own body. You may start thinking about writing your will, although in many cases this doesn't get done for a while yet. You spend a lot of time serving the crone, looking after her needs.

There is an added spirituality that comes to us with the loss of physical fertility, which deepens our psyches, brings up our anger, gives us a chance to conclude and complete what isn't yet finished in our lives. If you have been angry with a family member for a long time, or with an ex-lover, husband, or girlfriend, this is a good time to make up. The benefit of this arduous and sometimes embarrassing work is to integrate the lights and shadows of our personalities.

"Life is too short!" is no longer just a meaningless saying of the older generation. By now, illnesses and accidents may have taken loved ones from us. We understand in our hearts and have accepted the reality that life passes quickly. Why, you haven't even gotten to unpack all your baggage from the forties, and you are still carrying around some uncompleted dreams!

Don't fear the Fates, because they are your renewal. As you move into your fifties and beyond, you may separate out parts of your life that must be completed before you leave Verdandi. Your task is to distill the ego and share the wisdom and experience you have gained since your first Saturn return. We are called to teach the new generation now, share with others what we know. There are always a few whom we can save from some grief by mentoring.

Mother Jones, the legendary labor organizer, is a good example of how women may change at this time. She had lost her children and husband to sickness, her house had burned down in the great Chicago Fire, she had nothing more to lose. From this time on she never had a permanent address. She kept on moving—staying at people's homes, then moving on—and this is when she became such a fierce activist for the coal miners. She lived and worked tirelessly, helping the unions, organizing the wives to keep the scabs away. She transmuted her suffering and loss into a new life and a new destiny. Pain is often the messenger of destiny.

Sojourner Truth was especially active in her early fifties, touring the country, giving speeches. Southern sympathizers often tried to disrupt her meetings; she was clubbed in Kansas, mobbed in Missouri, accused of being a man at other times. She bared her breasts to prove she was a woman, and turned every attack on her to her own advantage. She became a Chiron, the wounded healer, traveling between the black and white worlds.

One of the karmic choices we make at this time is to seek healing or to heal others. Traditionally, the most effective healers are the old women, who not only remember the spells and recipes that modern science has forgotten, but have a lifetime of experience to guide them in deciding how to use them. Such healers are rare now.

WORKING: AN OLD HEALING RITUAL FROM HUNGARY

In rural Hungary there were few doctors but there were the *Vajakos asszony,* who knew the herbs, prayers, and rites. For infections and broken bones, people went to those who were available, but for most illnesses, first they saw the healer, then my grandfather. My grandfather Geza was a pharmacist, the closest thing to a professional doctor. He used to sew up the sliced-off ears of peasant boys after a night of fighting. But Victoria was the town's witch, to whom he himself went for help for more serious ailments. She would pray over her patients and pour melted beeswax into a bowl of water. The wax shapes that formed on the water told her whether her prayer would have good effects or not. Village healers specialized in psychic illnesses, diseases of the soul that they believed caused sickness in the body. Their logic was that sickness has to come from somewhere; therefore, it can be sent back, like an unwelcome visitor, to where it came from.

Many people got better by being prayed over in this way. After the prayers, the water would be sprinkled over the patient.

Because the Church forbade people from doing this healing ceremony, though, often they only performed it for family members, and in secret.

This forbidden ritual is done at the new moon, when there is a strong crescent. The healer brings a small tub of water and some melted beeswax in a pitcher. A white candle is lit.

When the healer is ready to pray from the heart, she enters a trance. The prayer trance is not deep but it is intense. A few breaths and her spirit links with the one who is ill to drive out the pain and suffering.

Anna, the Virgin, a grandmother, who in this poem represents the Fates, calls in the healing powers. Here is the prayer (to be sung to an improvised melody):

> *Up and past the seventh heaven*
> *grows the sacred cedar tree.*
> *The tree has three branches,*
> *each pointing to a destiny.* (Pour the wax into the water)
> *Saint Anna sits under the first branch.*
> *She gathers the sick to be healed.*
> *She removes the hurt, the suffering*
> *with the touch of her green silk.* (Pour out more wax)
> *Under the second branch is the Blessed Virgin.*
> *She cries with you and mourns and wails,*
> *she understands your problems,*
> *she will remove them day by day.* (Pour out more wax)
> *Under the third branch sits your grandmother,*
> *who has ministered to you before.*
> *She chases away the causes of the illness,*
> *calls your own body to be strong.* (Pour out more wax)

After you've finished the prayer, unfasten the patient's clothing so that the skin is exposed. Now take a flower and dip it into the water with the wax in it, and sprinkle it on the patient.

Here come the three sisters on your road of life. You say, "Hello" and they say, "What's wrong?"

You tell them, "Look, my friend here is sick and pained."

They say, "Not to worry, we are specialists in taking the pain away, because no sickness is more powerful than the Fates. No man or woman is as powerful as the Fates. Nothing can overrule us, no laws can disobey us, and we order that you'll be completely healed!

"Wholesome and healed. Wholesome and healed. Wholesome and healed . . ."

Now the patient is fully dressed again and put to rest. Keep a white candle burning in the room. Its flickering will remind you that the spirits are working on your behalf from now on. Burn a little sage to purify the room and to invite the healing angels to do their work.

HUNGARIAN FOLK-HEALING PRAYER

The rocks are cracked in time.
The dead will rise again in time.
I ask you, what are you afraid of?
Why do you shake? Tremble?
Oh dawn, pink dawn,
I was invited to a party
but I cannot go myself.
I'll send instead my shaking and trembling, my fever.
I'll send instead my sickness.
So mote it be!

THE RETURN OF SATURN

Between the ages of fifty-seven and fifty-eight, Saturn returns for the second time to the point on your chart it occupied when you were born. The mother of psychic balance has completed her second life lesson. Just when you've gotten a good grip on your Verdandi fate, it is the turn of the third Fate goddess, Skuld, to take over your life.

You feel your mortality, yet part of you has just really started enjoying life. There is less insecurity, fewer apologies, certainly less fear about the future. You have lived, you have survived. You know you will die. The end is the same for all. And now a certain "knowing" is developing within you. The old soul is awakening, and your crone fate is taking over the reins.

The good Fate Skuld has come to play with you. She has already begun to rearrange you physically via menopause. You are gaining strength as you fight your way through hot flashes, aches and pains, and whatever wounds still remain to heal after your Chiron return. Now she will design a new fate for you to follow, one more destiny for the road.

I am in this age group as I write this work, between fifty-seven and fifty-eight years old. I am beginning to relax at last about the progress of women's spirituality—all the signs are there that we are gaining. I used to be very intense, worrying so deeply that my message, which was the divinity of all women, would get drowned out, but not anymore. We women are holding on to our gains—not without a fight, of course, but that's okay. Women must learn how to fight for themselves as a group. Womanhood is beyond class and race, beyond east and west, north and south. Womanhood is a global phenomenon, its humanity.

As we grow older, it is even more important to celebrate our birthdays, starting with the fifty-eighth. This is the time to celebrate the second Saturn return, the passage from Verdandi to Skuld! All the other curves converge at this time of our lives. It is as momentous as the first Saturn return, but we are more prepared for it. Wisdom and peace of mind are coming. To some it will come in the form of business success; to others, in small pleasures, comforts, and life service. This transitional phase continues until around age sixty-three, when your new crone identity emerges.

WORKING: AN OPULENT PARTY

Since Saturn doesn't actually return to its original position until you are fifty-eight and three-quarters, Laurie's "Ops return" party was really a celebration of Verdandi, a thanks-giving for all that the Fates had brought into being for her during this part of her life, and maybe a little encouragement to them to keep doing it! You can use ideas for Laurie's party to create one of your own.

The dominant color at this party was Verdandi red, a deep, rich, crimson red, the color of red velvet. Laurie had borrowed a chair upholstered in that color from a friend who collects Victorian furniture and used it as her throne. She put a red damask cloth on the table, red candles in the polished brass candlesticks, and so forth. Guests were encouraged to bring red roses, which were placed in vases all over the room.

In mythology, the time when Saturn and Ops were the supreme god and goddess was called the Golden Age. During their reign, the weather was always perfect, and there were neither rich nor poor—people lived together in peace and equality. In ancient Rome, the equivalent of our Christmas season was Saturnalia. Like us, the Romans celebrated it with gift-giving and lots of parties, but during that time slaves had the rights of free men and were served by their masters. I bet that women also had more rights then also—a real Age of Gold!

Laurie made an altar to Ops, covered it with red velvet, and placed on it a statue of the Venus of Willendorf, and there was a wicker cornucopia sprayed gold, which she had filled with all kinds of fruit. Usually we think of the Willendorf goddess as a fertile earth mother, and that is true, but Susan Weed, my herbalist author and witch friend, has pointed out that the figure's pendulous breasts and sagging belly are more characteristic of a woman at the end of her fertile years who has already borne many children.

The altar was also draped with gold necklaces and a scattering of chocolate coins covered with gold foil. As each woman came in, she was given a red rose to lay on the altar.

The food, which was fabulous, was heavy on red items and chocolate. I particularly remember one raspberry torte, which I am convinced not only added a pound to my weight when I ate it, but is probably adding a few ounces just by being remembered! After we had eaten, everybody's glass was filled with either cranberry apple juice or a port dessert wine, and we made toasts to all the achievements of Laurie's Verdandi years.

Praise be for the blessings enjoyed in the past!

Praise be for the blessings received!

Praise be for the new blessings already on their way.

I hope the goddess was pleased. The rest of us certainly came away from the party with a cheerful glow.

Skuld

CHAPTER SEVEN

SKULD

I said
I would not
grow old.
Years later
I met
the Dearest Goddess.
I should
have known . . .
I had stepped
into
an old woman's
footsteps.

LATVIAN WOMEN'S FOLK POEM
NO. 3475 (1249)

Skuld and I walk together in the cemetery at least twice a week. She likes to hang out on the tombstones and rest her weary bones in the better mausoleums—she likes the ones overgrown with ivy best. There she sleeps or just floats in the wind until I come by, and then she catches up with me and my little Hungarian puli, Zoro.

She likes to pretend that she is interested in our friendship because of the dog.

"Hey you, little black puli dog, there you are, come play with me!" She emerges from behind the mausoleum and the dog picks up his head, all his nerves tensing in attention. Then he lets out a little bit of a bark, the high note he uses to greet special people. But this one is for the presence that often joins us when we reach the Hewitt plot; Skuld likes it because of the view.

Today the air has that tingling clarity that often comes in the autumn. The grass on the hills above the cemetery is ripe and golden, the sky a pale blue, mirrored by the deeper cobalt of the

Bay. But a wind of change is rustling in the eucalyptus trees, and the fir trees wave their branches black against the sky.

"Welcome, Spirit of Wisdom!" I greet her.

"What a fine, blessed day!" she says. "So how is my favorite little three-legged dog?"

"He is great—see for yourself—but he needs more exercise. He is always alone, with nobody to run with."

"Ah, you always bring this up. It wasn't my fault that his girlfriend Christy died. The kennels were at fault. They inbred the Tibetan terriers so much that the line developed genetic anemia and she didn't survive."

"Where do dead dogs go?"

"The same place people go. Home."

"Doggie heaven?"

"No, just heaven."

"Is it nice there?"

"It is blissful. You don't have the drugs on earth that can induce the bliss to be had in death."

"Really?"

"It's the best of the gifts we have. In death you rest up; you visit a lot; you have great learning experiences; you hang out with your role models; all is equal; all is calm. Democracy at its best."

"In heaven you have democracy?"

"Yes. And no discontent."

"No rebellion?"

She looks over the rows and rows of tombstones. "Never a rebellion," she whispers.

"Wow."

Then I think I am not sure I would fit in.

She hears my thought. "That's why you are not here yet."

The dog runs ahead and she chases him with little winds, throwing him a branch, which he catches proudly in his mouth and brandishes along the way back. Little Zoro loves to play with Skuld.

"How is the cemetery?" I ask.

"It's filling up! Every day new ones are arriving. The young dead come every day, sometimes more than one. They come in car caravans, and in limos, in rented hearses. The mourners pile out to put the body into the earth, stay a little bit, then they are gone forever. Look at these graves—nobody has tended them in years!"

"I like it like that," I say. "I like it honest. You are dead, you are out of the game. People don't visit a graveyard unless they have dogs to walk."

We watch a group of mourners gather. The pastor recites the familiar verses: ". . . Yea, though I walk through the valley of the shadow of death, I shall fear no evil."

As soon as the dirt has been thrown onto the casket, people start going back to their cars, moving awkwardly away, careful not to show disrespect. But the truth is, people are uncomfortable in cemeteries. Sometimes I see some joggers, but not many. It's just the dead, alone.

Again hearing my thoughts, Skuld says, "No, not alone. I am with them every day. And you, too. Are you going to read their names aloud as you pass the graves? The dead really appreciate that. Even when you mispronounce their names. At least they hear it. The very last mantra is one's name, one's identity."

"Okay," I say. "Let's see, here we have Mr. Hutch, Mr. and Mrs. Brandon, Mrs. and Mr. and three kids all named Jennison. And over there is Mother Wellingworth and the two little girls Eva and Madge. They were English."

"Good." Skuld is calling their names, too. She brushes her hands against the stones, as if reading the names with her fingers.

"Kraft . . . Bradbury . . . Delger . . . Powell . . . Stanyon . . ."

"What does it matter what your name was on the other side?"

"Don't you understand? Don't you want to know what branch of the Tree of Life you came from? That is the only topic on the other side! People like to gather all their relatives, wonder and marvel at the intricate interconnectedness of life and death.

"Caldwell . . . Peters . . . Harrison . . . Mable . . ."

The names call up little winds, as if the dead are laughing. My puli happily chases the winds, the flying leaves, the sticks and fallen fir cones, black dreadlocks bouncing on his little butt. He pirouettes on his one hind leg on a smooth tombstone that fell over in the wind of some storm.

"Oh, I love that little dog of yours! Bring him along again tomorrow!"

"I will!" I promise as I open my car door for the shaggy puli to jump in. "Say good-bye, Zoro!"

Skuld plants a kiss on his little domed head.

"Protect us!" I say.

"As always!" she replies.

And we roll out of Deathland, leaving the ghostly whitewashed forest of tombstones behind. As we speed through the gate we can see people there with placards, demonstrating against unfair hirings and firings and racism in the cemetery. Hmm . . .

Here is rebellion at the gates!

WHAT SHOULD BE SHALL BE

The third Norn likes to hang out in the graveyard, but that is not her only environment. Her name means "what shall be," and she rules the third destiny, the one that begins with the second Saturn return. She is the future. Of course, death is in the future for all of us, but in the normal course of things, we have at least thirty more years of life to get through before we're ready for the peace of the other side.

In Greek mythology, the third Fate is Atropos, the cutter. She is called "the Inflexible" because she is what must be. No exceptions.

She cuts the thread of life, but she also cuts the old strings that tangle us and hold us back as we continue to work out our destiny.

Never before has Skuld had so many playmates. The average life span, at least in the United States, has never been as long as it is now. At the turn of the century people barely made it past their fifties (except, of course, for the hardy few in my family who made it into their eighties, like my aunt Titi and my grandfather Zoltan; my own mother passed on at sixty-three). Today we often live into our nineties. My best friend's parents are in their late seventies and mid-eighties; another friend has a ninety-something stepfather and an eighty-something mother living in Florida. As new medical techniques are developed, we have the prospect of a cure for cancer by the end of the century, which will have a major positive effect on life expectancy.

Skuld stirs the cauldron, and cronehood grows in me like an egg. I look out and see wonderful signs that point way beyond my own lifetime and I am glad. I have already promised myself to come back in four or five hundred years, when we reach the true Age of Aquarius. Like the ancient Celts, who arranged to pay their debts in the next life, my soul is already making plans beyond this lifetime.

For my third destiny, I would like to get published in Budapest. I would have to drop "Budapest" as my last name, of course, since it would be redundant. I should think up a good crone name for my third fate's personality. Maybe my unusual middle name, Emese. Many dreams occupy me when I am walking—the crone clearly wants to have fun!

Who is Skuld? Scandinavia and Scotia are named after her. The goddess Skuld is actually a jolly Moira. It is true that she is the one who cuts the thread of life, but when the time comes, she is welcomed, as death ends the suffering of this life and opens the door to a new one.

She likes to ride out with the folks; she likes sports; she likes risky games. In Iceland, where her name is used daily, if you "Skuld" somebody, it means you owe something. We owe her our bodies back. The names of the Norns survived in Iceland, where Christianity could take hold only if it didn't attack the old goddesses. But her name means nothing frightening. It is what "must be."

The destiny that was yours to play out as an adult has been completed in Verdandi. If you get this close to Skuld, you have the opportunity to catch your "third wind," a new destiny. Skuld will offer you one more purpose, one more cause, one more game to participate in. Skuld writes with poetry and hymns and invocations, with paintbrushes and new loves. This is a time when a woman can find her true bliss, a higher self-esteem, a jelling of the mind. While still alive, she can manifest her fullness. Grandma Moses, the famous American primitive painter, discovered her talent in her late seventies. Skuld will not take you home unless you have done what you came here for and used your talents.

This third destiny is such a privilege! But you have to love the old woman. You cannot get hung up on Verdandi and try to stay young forever at all costs. You have to say good-bye to your unlined face and firm body. You have to say good-bye to your flexible joints. Like a tree, you will be cut down, and you know it. It is only a question of when. But we will enjoy our third destiny much more if we keep fit. We may not be up for the physical sports we enjoyed when we were younger, but if we are careful and build up strength and muscle tone gradually, we will maintain bone mass and vitality much longer. Skuld rides horses; we can bicycle, swim, walk, whatever—the point is we have to keep moving.

Throughout your life you have been watched over by the three Old Sisters. There may have been times when you've felt as if you've lost your way, but even that was part of the plan. *Qué será, será.* What has happened is what was meant to be. This is the way of Skuld.

And you're not finished yet. Skuld must dance with you one more time. Do you want another thirty years? Most people do, and with increasing life expectancies, you are likely to get it whether you want to or not! Whatever you denied yourself during your first two Fates, now is your time to have. Full personality reversals are possible. Docile little queens can and have suddenly gone radical. You see grandmothers demonstrating, sitting in trees protecting the earth. Doing conscientious work is a fine third mission. What, after all, do you have to lose?

Skuld is very powerful. It doesn't matter what age of the Earth you are living in, Skuld will bring about her changes. If you were a hardworking woman (and what woman isn't?), you may choose to slow down now and take it easy. Bake cookies. Astrology tells us that in this third Saturn cycle of our lives we get to relinquish our responsibilities as householders, or as the main earner in the family; we get to put down our burdens and relax.

A new spiritual identity will emerge from this stillness. If you already had a strong spiritual orientation, now you may deepen it and come to appreciate it more fully. If you never meditated in your life, if you floundered between sects and religions, if you were a self-taught pagan, now you'll come to a peaceful understanding that all religions are one. As Dion Fortune, the English author, puts it, "All gods are one God, and all goddesses are one Goddess, and there is one Initiator."

In this second initiation you are not so fearful. You may even find deep joy in this inner shifting. You have done it before—it's familiar. But back then you had to be dragged kicking and screaming into change by Verdandi—now you can look back with gratitude and see how that transformation played itself out, and look forward with hope, not fear, to the next one.

CRONEHOOD: THE TIME OF WISDOM

Crones can be powerful heads of state. Indira Gandhi was a crone when she was prime minister; so was Margaret Thatcher. Women in this age group can win elections, make good decisions, and wage their battles effectively. There is nothing a crone cannot achieve in Skuld.

My favorite role model for the third destiny is the fantastic suffragist Elizabeth Cady Stanton, whose first Saturn return I related in Chapter 4. Her crone career was born out of her first Saturn cycle career. At fifty-eight, she entered fully into the political movement, truly revealed her strength, and made a herstorical contribution. Opposed by husband and friends, even by her own father, she made a "fierce" decision to devote her considerable energy entirely to women's causes. She crisscrossed the country, giving speeches about equal rights for women: the right to control her own earnings (only males could receive and keep money back then), child care, education, entry to professions in the pulpit and the government. She braved hail and snow to keep her speaking engagements, sometimes when all the other speakers had canceled. At sixty-five, she hired horse-drawn sleighs if she needed them in order to fulfill her commitments. She was charismatic as a speaker and enjoyed the contact with her audience.

As a crone she was a radical. When the first centennial was celebrated by the whole country, she and Susan B. Anthony decided to crash the ceremonies, demanding the vote for women. While the self-congratulating ceremonies were in full swing around the Statue of Liberty, Susan and Elizabeth hired a small boat to circle the island, from which they broadcast their message of women's suffrage through a bullhorn, disrupting the smugness and orderliness of the celebrations.

At eighty she was honored in New York at the Metropolitan Opera House. All her life she had been opposed and vilified, but when she hit her crone's stride, the world could finally hear her. Her message—the importance of women's equality—had finally been understood. But Elizabeth didn't slow down. She started studying socialism, and the relationships between labor and capital, and finally she targeted the work that has most damaged the cause of women's rights—the Bible. For her efforts, the shortsighted leadership of the Women's Suffrage Association (which she had started) renounced her and cast her out. She collected ten women scholars who were experts in the languages in which the Bible had originally been written and they translated it from scratch, a ten-year project. The women discovered that paid clerks had translated the Bible.

In my play, *The Rise of the Fates,* these are the words I gave her to say, based on some of Elizabeth's speeches:

"My book, *The Women's Bible,* comes like a great benediction to women. It tells them that the Lord didn't write the book, that the garden scene is a fable, that women are in no way responsible for the laws of the universe. The Christian scholars and scientists would not tell her this, for they see she is the key to the situation. Take the snake, the fruit tree, and the woman out of the story and we have no fall, no frowning judge, no inferno, no everlasting punishment, hence no need for the Savior. Thus the bottom falls out of Christian theology!"

Elizabeth Cady Stanton died a year short of her fourth Saturn return; the Goddess collected her spirit, like a precious jewel. She was honored nationally as the grande dame of women's liberation.

FATE DATES OF SKULD

During the third Saturn cycle, we morph fertility into wisdom. Although age is not a guarantee of wisdom, it is hard to escape picking up some of it.

At around age sixty, we have a Jupiter return, a joyous expansion in which profound realizations are possible. Between the ages of sixty and sixty-two, Uranus returns to its natal position, just as it did when you were twenty-one and forty. This is a time for imagination, a prime time to write in your journal; creativity is stimulated now. If you stifle creativity, you get depressed, so don't. Your soulwork involves confronting your ideas about liberation and rebellion. We depend on you to be outrageous. We need to see the limits. It is still not too late. Our third fate is unfolding with this boost from Uranus. When we are sixty-three, this is an initiation for the journey home. Now we start thinking about retirement. We start contemplating a life beyond this one.

Between the ages of sixty-five and sixty-six, the structure of your life is again under reconstruction as Saturn again influences the first quarter of your Skuld cycle. Have you organized your use of energy well? You still have so much to do, establish, fund, even initiate. You must be sure you are comfortable when at rest. What does your body need for deeper stability? Get a nutritional evaluation and take supplements if necessary.

The seventies begin with the sixth Jupiter return, between the ages of seventy-one and seventy-two. This brings expansion of the mind and probably of the girth, too. Share what you have gained—sign up to read fairy tales to children, give some great parties, give gifts, and finalize your will. Jovial Jupiter loves social activities; take advantage of this energy and party. Seriously, though, it's time to acknowledge the deep wisdom you have gained about maturity. Does anybody in your family need your wisdom? We are all lucky to have you around.

Between seventy-two and seventy-three it is time to review the changes you made in your mid-sixties. You need to refurbish the structure that holds your life. Is it good enough? Saturn contemplates the approach of death and makes peace with it. Your body is more demanding, needs more time to maintain. Be aware of the kinds of issues about authority that emerge in your life now.

In our later seventies we begin to look within. For some, these are hermetic years; for others, soulwork is communal. Between the ages of seventy-five and ninety-four a full cycle occurs, a time of life yet to be experienced by the soul-conscious generation. We usually return to some form of spirituality if we haven't already.

If you make it to your eighties, it is time to reflect on the changes you made in your early seventies. What other aspects of the external world can you let go of? How can you move deeper into the eternal foundations of your spirit? How can you recognize more deeply that we are not just our bodies but eternal souls as well? Spirituality will really work now if you have developed it already. Your prayers are powerful, your spells all go home. You are getting closer to the Fates.

In the early eighties, we are again under the influence of Neptune. This always indicates a time of high energy for creativity. Meditate, sleep in the afternoons, dream, write. Keep active and eat right. A crone's life must be restful, but it still needs a little mission now and then. Your soulwork is to confront the dreams you have now—your illusions, your favorite obsessions—and let go of some of them. Surrender more to the organic rhythms of your body and reflect on self-forgiveness.

Between eighty-three and eighty-four, the seventh Jupiter return energizes expanding mind and heart. What opportunities for expanding your beliefs and sharing your wisdom are now here?

THE FOURTH FATE

Traditionally, humans were allotted threescore and ten years—that is, seventy. These days, it is far more likely that you will at least make it to your eighty-fourth year and your third Saturn return. There have always been some remarkable souls that made it past this point, but now we all can look forward to considerable numbers. What does the fourth Saturn cycle have in store?

For many, this fourth destiny is the time when we at last have the leisure to take stock, to evaluate what we have done with our lives and try to understand it, and then to let go. We have paid our dues, done our duty, earned money, borne children, taken responsibility for others. Now at last we have the leisure to "make our souls."

Skuld's dance is done. Another thirty years have passed. Now it's time to retire. Hang out, meditate, eat good foods, be moody, even cantankerous. You have lived a long and good life; now entertain yourself. Even soulwork becomes a simple delight. Go on automatic. Your next phase in life will take you home.

Eighty-four brings the famous "second wind," the Uranus return. If you reach it, your mind will jell with new clarity. It is time to honor the uniqueness you carry and recognize how you have lived your life according to your own terms. If not, change it. When my aunt Titi reached this age, she stopped snoring, her memory returned, and she spoke faster and better and more.

Between eighty-five and eighty-six, we are influenced by Pluto. This is an opportunity to confront death on another level of intimacy. How can you feel empowered in the process of preparing for it? Review and honor the parts of your life that will continue after you are gone, such as children and grandchildren, works of art, memories.

After you pass eighty-four, kick back, for heaven's sake, and write your memoirs!

Mother Teresa was a living crone in our times. Her first opus, the Order of the Missionaries of Charity, became a pontifical order (very rare—she had only the Pope to answer to) when she was only fifty-five—a Verdandi achievement. Within its walls the sole objective is to give love without religious instructions. Up to her death at the age of eighty-seven, she worked with the most desperate people on earth—people with AIDS, lepers, and children from the streets of Calcutta. She spoke to queens, kings, and dictators alike, seeking help for the poor, and was a recipient of the Nobel Prize. Her order continues to carry on her mission of love and equality for all in the poorest neighborhoods.

My own approaching cronehood is unfolding. Many things that were very important to me before have become quite incidental.

Other things that I thought I had forgotten have emerged as a focus of attention.

I used to like to travel a great deal, giving workshops, but now I dread having to pack my bags and get on the road. I only go if I am really taken care of. I have started thinking about my friends differently, wanting to spend more social time with them. I realized that all my life I have bonded only through work. I question that now. I am one of those who can give a good time, but slowly I have forgotten how to have a good time. As of this writing, I am moving into my fifty-eighth year, and my Verdandi mission consisted of so much fun work to pursue that I got out of the habit of just playing.

I marked this passage with a croning ceremony held in June 1996, at the second biannual International Goddess 2000 Festival. A croning ritual is an initiation into the third Skuld fate. This is an important event; you must treat it with the utmost respect. It is a party with a theme—saying good-bye to your youth. During the second Saturn return the women turn into crones and the men into cronies. The process begins at age fifty-six, but Saturn does not return completely to the natal point and complete its return until you are fifty-eight. Any time during this period when you feel that the transformation is well under way, you can call your friends together for a croning ritual.

Be clear about what it is you are doing. I cannot stand it when older women are lied to: "Oh, you are still young at heart," "You still look young!" or "You just have to keep young thoughts in your head." That is crap. Women need to accept themselves as older women. We are not benefiting from being fed delusions. Everyone gets old if they are lucky, even if they have the money to try to defy the process through plastic surgery every other year. If you don't like getting old, just think of the alternative!

My croning ritual was held outdoors: Imagine a large fire circle in the Indian Bowl, a kind of Greek theater and the conference center. I had a hard time saying good-bye to Verdandi, so for my ceremony, I had to go down into the bottom of the theater and circle the huge sacred fire of life, casting into it tokens of Verdandi, talking to her gently while I walked around the fire.

At first I thought I would be all right. Calmly I walked down the wooden steps to the center of the circle. I shivered a little when the priestess removed my queenly flower crown and placed the mask of the white wolf over my head (the white wolf, like all canines, is sacred to the Fates). But for the most part I still felt as I would during any other ritual, serious and respectful. The true impact came later.

As I slowly walked around the huge bonfire, I imagined that the circle was my life. I walked the childhood path, the adolescent path, the way of adulthood, because I certainly had a big reversal in Verdandi. I walked through the shimmering air, the heat of the fire burning my arms. Many things I cast away, but I still clutched my beloved little voodoo doll that represented me in all my doings. The doll was my little teacher, my golden attractor, the doll with which I had cast spells upon myself for years. She was green-limbed, had my own white hair on her head, gold dust on her nose. She represented me in Verdandi.

Then I turned the corner. Suddenly the circle of life was diminishing. I saw that my life was mostly over and all that was left was the last Fate. This shocked me. I tried to say the words:

"Good-bye, Verdandi! Good-bye, my youth! Good-bye, my middle age! Welcome the crone!"

But then I started sobbing. This is when you feel it. My wolf mask wobbled as I cried, but I didn't care. I stayed there and had a good cry. Then I walked around the rest of the circle, the other side. I cast cinnamon sticks into the sacred fire to help bring in good luck. When I finished my ritual, I felt as if I had taken a physical journey; I was exhausted and triumphant to have made it to the other side. I wept some more.

At least the mask was giving me some privacy in this huge circle of women. A wrenching sob came up—a sound I had never heard myself make before. It was heartrending. Why did I so hate to say good-bye to Verdandi? I've always honored the crone, and I've been looking forward to my cronehood for a long time. But when it came right down to accepting it, I felt pain.

I was mourning my elastic limbs, my endless strength that would allow me to climb mountains and worship all night with dancing and song, then get up early in the morning and be out there doing my work by six A.M. All that loving, too—all that passion now has mellowed. Sex isn't all-important anymore. Friends and laughter have moved up in importance on my list of values. Something had been happening, all right. This was no joke.

But I got through it somehow. And when the keepsakes had turned to ashes, and the tears had dried, I felt a great freedom. Rituals are essential to communicate with our own souls.

CRONING RITUAL

You don't have to have a circle of a hundred women to honor this passage. Celebrate yourself with a ritual at home, either outdoors or in your living room. Get a special ring to represent you as a crone. A deep amethyst would be good—purple is the color of success and completion.

When the moment is right, get everybody's attention. Start with a little speech, which can be given by your best friend and should go something like this:

> Hello, everybody. Thank you for coming to help us reclaim croning as the new women's ritual. We celebrate the life of [fill in your name], who has reached her fifty-eighth year [or your age], a turning point. We honor her with this ring because today it is her turn to accept the

responsibilities and honors of the crone. In ancient times old women were the carriers of culture and values, protectors of the young. Today the culture denies us our respectful lined faces and our achievements in having built and strengthened the human family.

[Name], I would like to present to you this crone jewel to remind you of this day. Whenever you look at it, remember that you are our beloved sister, teacher, and now an honored crone of the Goddess.

When you put on the ring, let your friends ring a bell fifty-eight times, once for each year you have lived. While you are listening to the many bells, silently say good-bye to those years, then bless and release them. If the setting allows you to have a fire, you can throw symbols of the Verdandi Fate that you are releasing onto the flames as I did.

Light as many candles as you have years and don't blow them out, let them burn down naturally. Just as at a "fate date" birthday party, tell stories from your life while your guests are having cake and wine. Give the leftovers to stray dogs as a service to the Fate goddess Skuld, to whom dogs are sacred.

The same sort of ritual can work for celebrating a man's entry into the "crony" phase of life as well, perhaps substituting a pendant or other symbol for the ring. Don't forget that both sexes comprise the human race—beloved fathers turn into grandfathers and beloved partners turn into white-haired companions.

Stepping into cronehood involves an inner shift for a different destiny. It is time to think about how we are going to provide for the crone. The crone likes nice things; she likes her creature comforts; she likes happy people around her, love, and even some part of mothering if there are grandchildren. It is time to put money aside, make plans for the future. We can no longer assume we will have only a few years after retirement. With current life expectancies, we may have to support ourselves for thirty years longer.

In the croning ritual we receive a crone jewel that signifies our new status as an elder. I recommend taking a crone name as well. In some societies, people take new names with each stage of life. We are many people throughout our lives—why should our names remain the same?

CHAPTER EIGHT

DEATH

Dearest Goddess,
if you are
going to meet
the Unwelcome Goddess,
why not meet her
on the bridge?
I will walk by
and push
the Unwelcome Goddess
into
the river.

LATVIAN WOMEN'S FOLK POEM
NO. 9188.224.109, 335

My mother visited with dead people all the time. My mother was a big dreamer. In her dreams she would meet friends who had died many years before and spend a couple of pleasant hours with them. These visits then became food for conversation for the rest of the day.

This is what she knew.

Death is a state of being. No time exists there, no sense of change. Everything has stopped. However, the souls could present themselves in any shape they pleased in order to reveal themselves to her in her dreams. The dead would come by to enjoy the birdsong, just like Mom. Sometimes the dead appeared to be bothered by some unfinished business from their lives. Money matters were common, especially if people had hoarded money in secret, saving it for a rainy day. If they died suddenly, they would realize that they had never told their heirs where the money was, so Mom would pick up the message and pass it along to the relatives. Her morning phone calls included such mopping-up tasks, a result of the duties she had taken on while asleep.

A conversation might go like this:

"Hello, Kati, it's me. I dreamed of your husband last night."

"You saw my Jozsi last night? What was he doing, for heaven's sake?"

"He was giving me a message for you, Kati. Listen good! Jozsi told me he hid some money in the shed behind the house. It's in a green box, and it's against the wall, out of sight. He wants you to find it and use it."

"Is that all he wanted?" the widow would cry.

"No, of course not. He misses you very much. He said to enjoy life and that he loves you."

"Thank you!"

And Kati would go look in the shed and the money would be there.

So there does seem to be evidence that there is an afterlife, according to Mom, and a vigorous one at that. Does this mean, then, that death doesn't exist at all, there are just two different kinds of life?

No. Death is real. Death is more real than we admit in our culture. Death is more real than life because it lasts much longer. But both states are temporary. And then there is the third state of being, the world of the Fates, where we visit before reentering life and starting a new cycle.

Death is every day. Death is in small and larger doses. Death is the food we eat. We borrow our lives from death. Death feeds us while we live. Death eats us when we die.

NECESSITY: THE FINAL TURN OF THE WHEEL

Death is the mother of all the Fates. She is Necessity. What must be must be. Your death date was included in the birth date when you first entered this world. You always knew she would come. Now she is here.

From her presence life gains its meaning. She is meaning. She is the force that shapes the universe. Death and life are complementary; their cycle is the legendary Ouroburos, the serpent that encircles the world, biting its own tail. Death believes in equal opportunity; everyone has to go through that door. We see others going through it, in our dreams we understand it, our souls feel its presence, but we cannot see through it with our waking eyes. All our science cannot prove or disprove whether there is anything on the other side.

What if there is nothing? Do we simply break down into our component parts like any other organic matter? Do we have one shot at conscious life and then become elements that, after millions of years, are recycled into another life? Or is death a place, and in this place we have another kind of existence? We have all imagined it. Throughout human history, different cultures and religions have described it in their own ways. In Western civilization we inherit the Christian model of heaven and hell: the former if you have been good in this life and the latter if you've been evil, with purgatory thrown in for those who don't quite qualify for one or the other extreme.

The pagans believed that everybody, no matter what they had done in life, passed through death and change in the otherworld. The Egyptian *Book of the Dead* was a guide to the soul's progress. After death, the soul was weighed to determine its tally of good and evil. Understanding the meaning of its deeds, it would weep for its evils. It passed through a series of gates and encountered a sequence of judges, continuing in its progress toward becoming one with Osiris, where it would see the past through God's eyes.

Both the Celts and the Norse believed in reincarnation, especially when dead relatives were thought to have returned to the same family line. But some of the dead continued in the otherworld as guardian spirits. Especially powerful were the "disir," the spirits of maternal ancestors who continued to watch over the family.

Death is the famous space between the worlds, the world where sacred awe silences us in mute adoration. This space is the place we are seeking when we pray. It doesn't matter what word your language uses for God, or what religion you follow—when you pray deeply, you go beyond culture; with your body and mind you are reaching for this sacred space where the force that is one and then three all at once waits for you. This is where mystery lives.

ANCESTRAL SPIRITS

After my grandmother's death she became the guardian of the family. Grandmother died of hunger during the war. When alive she was a very sane and no-nonsense type of woman, always focused on practical solutions to problems. She raised funds and opened schools for girls to learn marketable skills.

She appeared to me in the moment of her death. I was almost three years old, when the spirit is active. I saw Grandmother and heard her voice. I was outside in the garden. I had colored little cotton balls red with ground-up brick dust and hung them on the bushes all over the garden. I don't know why I played this, but I remember death was all around me—this was during the war. And then I saw Grandmother descend from the sky. She floated over to me with her arms outstretched and embraced me, and as she did, she said, "My dear Zsuzsika, you won't have your dear old grandmother anymore!" We both wept. I felt it was a good-bye. She kissed me and said, "You be good girl, and I'll look after you, don't worry!" Days later a telegram finally reached Mother, announcing Grandmother's death in the exact hour that I saw her.

The second time she appeared was when I was nine years old. It was in my mother's apartment in Zuglo early one Sunday morning. This time her presence was accompanied by a deep chill. I was in bed next to Mom, and I woke up because I suddenly felt cold. Mother sat up, intently listening. Her lips were parted; she was paying rapt attention to something near the yellow stove. Then I saw it, too. Grandmother's image was not much bigger than a portrait painting, but her lips were moving as she whispered to Mom. I could not make out what she said, but I knew Mom could.

"What is it?" I asked her.

"It is Grandma, darling. Shh!"

When the apparition finished communicating, Mother jumped out of bed and insisted that we both get dressed and go over to see Titi, her sister, because, as my mother said, she had taken those funny pills again and was dying. We took a cab and knocked on Titi's door. There was no answer, but Mother had the key, so we let ourselves in. Titi was sleeping and we couldn't wake her up. We took her to the hospital where she worked as a pharmacist and there they pumped her stomach. My aunt had suffered from depression all her life, so this was not completely unexpected. But she did recover and is still alive.

This experience proved to me that the dead are watching us. Concerned parents don't stop being concerned just because they have passed on.

Recently I dreamed that Titi, now my only living older relative, was packing her bags again. Mother and Grandma and even Grandpa Geza were watching Titi pack. Then I heard them say:

"Not yet, Titi, there is a lot of room in there yet. You're not finished."

Titi will soon be eighty-three. I have a feeling she will be around for a while longer.

A SPECIAL GIFT

We all share the same fate in the end.

Once upon a time, in the elder age of Greece before the fall of Troy—an age when the Great Goddess still reigned supreme— three novice priestesses came to a remote cavern in the windswept mountainside to pay their respects to the Fates, and to bring their first offerings to the Old Ones. As they entered the cavern's somber depths, they bore baskets of red apples, knowing the Gray Ones relished red foods, for red is potent with life-giving magic. When they came to the altar, they found it veiled in mystery by the steamy breath of the goddesses' underground waters. They were full of fearful awe. Fervently they began chanting their prayer:

"Dearest Fates, Oldest of the Old, you who birth us in hope, you who wisely measure the threads of our lives, you who mercifully lay us out: Give us the best fate ever!"

With this, they spread out their sheepskins and prepared to sleep the night cradled in the Creatrix's womb.

At dawn, the aged priestess who was keeper of the shrine wondered why the playful young ones did not emerge, laughing and singing. As she braved the gloom, grim thoughts crowded closer with every step. When she came to the altar, she sank to her knees in horror. The soulless bodies of the three priestesses lay like discarded rags upon the stone, their empty eyes gazing out peacefully on the best fate known to woman or man.

Death.

This story comes to us as an explanation of how the Fates view death. It is quite the opposite of the Christian view: "The wages of sin is death," they drone. Excuse me—the wages of life is death. We all die. Even the saints. In fact, the good often die young. So what does that mean? I see everybody, priest and sinner, women and men, all come obediently to the gardens of Skuld.

Death is the other side of the same door. One side says "Enter" and the other says "Exit." Western culture fears death. We do many things to avoid it. Because there are doors between the worlds of the dead and the living, some people like to visit back and forth. Some never go near them. North Americans rarely visit their dead in the cemetery.

Western culture is not only afraid of death but also of the dead themselves. Our horror movies show how we dread decomposing bodies, how we fear the other side. We must make entertainment out of it in order to think about it at all. Asians, on the other hand, usually believe in the reincarnation of souls—in other words, the bodies may die, but the spirit is free to come back—and so it's very different in their part of the cemetery. In the Asian and Latino cemetery areas, the family comes out on holidays. They leave Christmas trees and poinsettias; for the children, always windmills and different toys. Sometimes they leave pumpkins on Halloween, and of course birthdays are remembered with fresh flowers. The Asian and Latino grave sites are tended much better than the Anglo ones. It is because of the difference in philosophy, not because white people don't love their dead. They just love them with fear, and not in the cemetery. Asian people see the cemetery as just one of the meeting points—a *quiet place to visit.*

Death delivers us from pain, when our bodies no longer work as they once did. And it brings us peace unutterable, as the ancient prayer promises. But it's another story when you try to imagine what happens on the earthly side; how the world you knew will change, how your relatives will forget you, and how, if you were buried in the unendowed section, in a hundred years or even less, the graveyard director may order the dirt to be turned over to make room for the new dead. For even the grave is not forever; even it changes, "dies," and gives way to the new.

THE FATES AND THE MYSTERY OF DEATH

According to astrology, in our birth charts there are several death nodes. These nodes are near the changing of the Fates, when we pass from Urdh to Verdandi, or from Verdandi to Skuld. These are points at which we can choose to make an exit or hang in there. If we struggle through, we can proceed to the next node, until one of them takes us down. My own mother departed when she reached her second death node.

These nodes are different for each person, and then, of course, there are accidents. Death can come at any time. The date of your death is included in your birth date. The number of heartbeats you will have has already been measured out to you. The measurers, the Moirae, established this at your birth.

Those two dates on your tombstone, birth and death, are your fate dates. In between fit all your laughter and tears.

Sometimes the Fates come for you when you are blooming in your youth. Children can die, even infants. But often the fate date coincides with one of your Saturn returns.

Janis Joplin and Jimi Hendrix, for example, both died at twenty-seven, just before their first Saturn return. It's almost as if when Urdh is reaching out to Verdandi to pass along a soul for a second Fate, something happens and it slips out and into the hands of Skuld instead. I have noticed this with other people as well. But when I looked at these two wonderful artists, it occurred to me that they had already achieved their fulfillment in the first Fate—they had influenced millions, marked the musical expression of their times. They came, they gave all, then they left.

These are the mysteries of death. No matter how I study it, I will never be able to come up with a "rule" that applies to all. Death has no rules. Skuld is an improviser.

When we consider people who have met violent deaths, we ask, Was that fate? Or was it an improvisation on the part of Death? That is, you showed up at the wrong place in the wrong time, and Skuld took you down. It is a mystery.

Sometimes the responsibility for death seems to be shared fifty-fifty with the Fates. Had Janis not taken an overdose of heroin, if Jimi had stayed clean, they could have lived longer. But they checked out at their first death node. At other times it is the manner of death that gives meaning to the life. Joan of Arc was a fiery teenager, touched by angels. She was dead at nineteen, her entire destiny played out in the five years between the time she left the

French countryside and when she was burned to death as a witch, having helped to win independence for her country. If the Church had not burned her, she might have been forgotten, despite her deeds, but because she was martyred, she became the patron saint of France.

Sometimes meaning can be found in an unjust killing. The killing of nine-year-old Polly Klass by an unrepentant ex-convict raised consciousness about the danger sexual predators pose to children, and laws in the United States have changed because of it—Megan's Law, for instance. It seems that civilization's advances are bought and paid for with the lives of the innocent. Human beings must get really horrified by their own evil in order to change. The survivors are saddened and outraged at death. Skuld is kind and caring to all the murdered bodies and departing souls. Once people are dead, Skuld leads them gently home. According to Hungarian mythology, when the west wind blows, it's a good time to die.

This I believe—that the experiences reported by people who have been clinically dead and then revived can tell us something real about what happens after the dearest body breaks down. After the heart stops, many people report a vision of white light. A tunnel, a way to the other side, opens up, then the figure of a guide, in a form determined by the individual's own religious beliefs, appears. Dead relatives extend smiling greetings. Often the soul is given the choice of returning to life or checking out now. Even then the soul is regarded by the Fates respectfully by being allowed the last choice. Do bad people go to hell? We wish. The angel offers an opportunity for self-judgment. The soul weeps for its evil doings. Hell is within. The inner reality travels with you wherever you are.

The mythology of the Fates tells us about the river where we drink the waters of life and forgetfulness. We become part of the fertile past, and as such, we nourish all the living. But when we have rested and healed, our souls may wake up and develop a desire to live again.

THE ART OF DYING

The dying often see through the veil between life and death. When my mother was just a few days from her death, she saw faces floating by, curiously checking her out, some smiling, some just watching. She believed that they were the guardians from the other side keeping an eye on her. She also heard crashing sounds in the middle of the night—huge noises, as if mirrors, or some of her ceramics, had been broken. But the morning revealed no damage, and no rational explanation for the sounds. She said it was the sound of the door between life and death being pushed open. We had to accept this because Mother was always right about the other side. She was no first-timer; she had visited the dead in her dreams many times.

If we are fortunate, we have warning when death is near, and if we have learned not to fear it, we can prepare. Death, like birth, is a process for which one can practice. Read the books by Elisabeth Kübler-Ross and others that recount near-death experiences. Imagine yourself going through the process until it no longer seems frightening.

If you have the privilege of assisting at the passing of a friend or loved one, there are a number of things you can do. Make the environment positive by keeping a lot of fresh flowers in the room. The custom of giving flowers to the sick comes from early burial practices. Flowers represent the Goddess as the life force; flowers give spiritual energy to the dying. If you know what kind of music the dying person finds soothing, or can ask, play it.

In Tibetan tradition, passages from the *Book of the Dead* are read to remind the soul of what it will need to do. Others may prefer to read psalms or poems. Even if someone is in a coma, they may be able to hear. And in any case, putting your thoughts into words helps you to focus and transmit them. Talk quietly about the good times you shared, and calmly come to closure on any issues that remain between you, even if you have to do it without apparent response.

Forgive and let go. When death is imminent, focus your thoughts on loving, supportive energy.

There are also things you should not do. When a person is dying, do not stage big scenes in the room, with outward displays of grief and sobbing and other dramatics. Avoid anything that produces fear and hooks the dying person into trying to hold on. Say goodbye serenely, without fear. Hold the person's hand or kiss her—and whatever you do, don't scream "Don't leave me!" unless you want to create a ghost.

My friend Marija Gimbutas, the famous goddess archaeologist, used to call me on serious matters. Our relationship took place on the phone for the most part; we met only a few times in real life. When she was first diagnosed with cancer of the stomach, the witches gathered and performed a huge healing ceremony for her, which actually helped to lengthen her life long enough for her to finish one more book.

She told me, "Oh, Z, I have so much more to say!"

"Then say it, Marija," I said. "Finish the work that keeps you here."

A few years later when the last book had come out, her autobiography was finished, the documentary was filmed, she called again.

"Oh, Z, it hurts so much. I am in so much pain," she said then.

"I am so sorry. . . ."

"My friends are doing another big healing ceremony for me."

"Do you want them to succeed?" I asked.

"I don't know. It just hurts so much. I cannot eat. . . ."

"Marija, did you say all you had to say?"

"Yes. I finally think I have."

"Then go home, priestess of the Goddess. You have given us all you had. Your mission has been accomplished. There is no need to suffer anymore."

There was silence on the other end of the line. Most of the women around her didn't talk to her this way.

Finally she spoke again. "Thank you, Z." I heard a big sigh. Her voice was more cheerful as she added, "Blessings to you!"

"Blessed be!" I replied.

Marija died on Candlemas, two days after we talked. So typical, she waited for the high holiday of Initiation (February 2) to exit into her new life.

I felt quite guilty about this for a while.

Everybody who had "worked" on her "cure" was proud of how they'd added years on her life. I was the death priestess who said it's okay to go. It's time. I didn't say to her, "Don't die, we need you, let us all pour our magic into your body, let's revive you one more time." I gave her "permission" to leave us.

Sometimes the best gift you can give to someone is to let them go. This is a necessary job when you are helping somebody to die. Somebody has to say, "You have done well, we all appreciate you, we thank you, but you don't need to suffer for us anymore. Go now. Go home."

WORKINGS: DEATH RITUALS

I have written about death rituals in more detail in my *Holy Book of Women's Mysteries*. These are the important things to remember.

If the loved one is unconscious, it doesn't mean she cannot hear you. She is listening with her soul, so your job is to fill her up with positive images, along with a little guidance on how to make her exit. It is helpful to pray to the goddess of death, to Skuld. Or Kali. Or the Black Madonna.

Here is a prayer based on some ancient prayers to Kali. Kali is the Hindu goddess who destroys in order to create.

> *I take refuge in her, Mother of all beings*
> *Who exists in all things in the form of power.*
> *Queen of the universe art thou, and its guardian.*

> In the form of the universe thou art the maintainer,
> By all the women thou art worshiped,
> As thy daughters we have great devotion to thee.

Here are some other prayers for the dying.

> You are the Earth, Creatrix of the world,
> You are Water,
> and in the form of Diana preserve the world.
> You are fire, and in the form of Pele build and destroy the world,
> You exist in the form of Isis,
> You are the air of the world.

> You are the primeval and auspicious one
> Mother of all men, refuge of your women
> Whoever moves in the changes of the world.
> The supporter of all, yet yourself without support
> The only pure form in the form of ether
> Oh, Mother Kali, be gracious to me!

> You are intelligence and bliss, a light yourself
> How, then, can I know you?
> Oh, Mother Kali, be gracious to me!
> You are that which supports and yet is not supported
> You pervade the world.
> You are in the form of the world
> That is pervaded by you.

> You are both negation and existence
> Oh, Mother Kali, be gracious to me!
> You are the atom, and ever pervading
> You are the whole universe.
> No praise is sufficient, yet your qualities prompt me
> To praise you!
> Oh, Mother Kali, be gracious to me!

BURIAL RITES

When they bring the body to the cemetery, the caravan of cars and limousines moves very slowly. But not really slow enough. The soul without the body is fragile and slow. Sometimes it takes a while for the spirit to realize that it has left the body and it's time to depart this world. If the soul hasn't already "gone home" to the lap of the Goddess, to meet all the other ancestors, then it hovers around the body. Loud noises and emotional storms can blow it miles away. It is a very bad idea to have gun salutes to the dead. The souls of the dead are still hovering around, finishing saying their good-byes, slowly letting go. With something like a gun salute, instead of being lovingly honored, these poor souls feel pushed away like evil spirits on a Chinese New Year. The twenty-one-gunshot salute blasts them all the way to the North Pole. It may take years for them to figure out what happened.

In some traditions the body is kept for three days before cremation or burial while prayers are chanted so that the hovering spirit will understand what has happened and what to do. Hospitals, of course, want the bed for another patient as soon as possible, but in a hospice, the family may be allowed to sit with the body for several hours. If someone dies at home, you can keep the body for up to twenty-four hours (depending on the weather), and perform your own rituals to honor it.

To send the dead to the grave bathed in chemicals, in full makeup, made to look as if she is not only alive but twenty years younger (with a fine tan), is ghoulish and anti-spirit. You should bless a basin of water, and with your hands over it say your blessings as you know them; perhaps float some flowers in the water, and bathe the body. This is the time when the spirit says good-bye to its longtime partner, our beloved spouse, the body. Getting it ready for burial should not be delegated to beauty professionals, but done by loved ones.

Do not allow the spirit to get unhappy because the body is going home. The soul, and the angel who guided this precious body, love this faithful spouse. If you keep watch beside the dead, you will notice a gradual transformation. At first she looks asleep, but as the remaining life energy departs, it becomes ever clearer that the body is now emptied of the animating spirit material, ready for the grave-yard, where it will become a blossom of bone. Say good-bye to it and give it back to the earth. Find a funeral home that will give you the simplest coffin possible. You don't want the dearest body to stay in an impenetrable coffin forever instead of blending gently with the earth. Unfortunately, most county regulations will not allow you to bury people in a burlap sack or a plain pine box.

I, of course, am of the fire school of burial: Burn the body and scatter the ashes, which is clean, not expensive, and natural.

DEVOTIONS TO THE DEAD

Devotions to the dead are actually for the living. The dead person is gone, but the living need to contemplate death in order to find meaning in life. Meaning, the third component of the universe, comes from death. Meaning informs the universe. From meaning comes insight. Only once we understand how transient all of our rushing about, our achievements and failures are, can we truly appreciate all we received. In retrospect, the most mundane aspects of our lives become huge gifts of brilliance and unimaginable rarity.

Think back to a time when you lost someone you loved, and how you regretted not having spent more time with her, how you could have just kicked yourself for not having written more often, visited longer, kept in touch. You realized your parents were not immortal; the strongest of your supporters gave way; your eternal lover had left you. All that you had was a small time and space to share, into which you had to cram all the living you could. Here is a prayer for the deathbed to the Fates themselves. Read this softly to the dying person if she cannot repeat your words.

> *Come to me,*
> *My powerful mothers,*
> *Come to me, you holy three!*
> *Nobody is more powerful than you are.*
> *You keep evergreen the very Tree of Life,*
> *you water the roots of my nature,*
> *you make my eyes shine,*
> *you make my soul rise in hope.*
> *Come to me, my three mothers,*
> *Stand at the bed and heal me*
> *or receive me into your bountiful laps.*
>
> *Three angels watch over me.*
> *One is protecting me,*
> *the other is guarding me,*
> *the third one is waiting*
> *to fly my soul home.*
>
> *I don't mind going home, my mothers,*
> *I don't mind living when you breathe with me,*
> *I don't mind dying if you die with me,*
> *I don't mind leaving if you fly with me.*
> *Receive me home with my wings spread wide.*
> *Save me, mothers, or cut me down,*
> *let my suffering cease.*
> *As you will it shall be.*
> *Blessed be!*

THE TREE OF LIFE UNDER HER WINDOW

Good morning,
Dearest Goddess.
Have you seen
my bride?
Yes.
She's on
the other side
of the river
in a wild patch
of blooming
roses.

LATVIAN WOMEN'S FOLK POEM
NO. 42976.378

The first exposure I had to the concept of the Tree of Life was in fairy tales. There were magical trees that sheltered people in their trunks overnight; there were trees that bore golden apples and silver pears. Some trees had dryads in them. Some trees could turn into women. Trees could do anything, transform everything, help any problem. I always respected trees as magical beings. Today I know trees to be the lungs of the planet. They are the soul of nature as well. In Native American lore trees are the arbiters between heaven and earth.

In the mythology of Scandinavia, all the worlds, all dimensions of existence, are arranged upon the branches of the World Tree, Yggdrasil, which grows beside Urdh's well. That well contains all the past, the entire history of all nations, even of the planet itself.

All that has ever lived is included in this essence. Some say that Yggdrasil is a stately ash tree, and others believe it is the long-lived yew. It symbolizes all that lives. The Norns water the tree every day. Skuld gathers clay from around the well, mixes it in with the sacred waters, and sprinkles it on the tree. This keeps it ever green.

Hungarian fairy tales love to start with the Tree of Life. The tree is the human family, and you are only the last little green leaf fluttering in the sun. The trunk of the tree is your species, the branches are your family. Our ancestors honored the dead because they knew that the dead are the roots through which we draw energy from the past. You feel the passion your uncle George once had for politics, you have a knack for gardening like your aunt Julie, you can cook like your mother did. The sap is drawn by Necessity all the way to the top of the tree, to you.

And what do we, the living, do for the dead? We interact with the world for them, we perform the all-important social photosynthesis, we create energy from what we take in from the outside world and send it back down to the roots. The Tree of Life is eternal. Evergreen. We water it daily by remembering, manifesting the dead. What is remembered lives.

Just as your ancestors were once alive and now are the roots of your being, so you, too, shall be transformed one day. There is no fear of death here, no fear of becoming invisible. The Tree of Life is all-inclusive.

In fairy tales, the Tree of Life grows under the "window"—the place from which we view the outside world. But so long as we stay by the window, we cannot tell what fruit the tree will bear.

What am I supposed to do with my life? Why am I here? What am I doing? These are questions I get from my clients all the time.

We spent little time in wondering about the purpose of life when we were children because we were close to the tree, and we knew that simply "being" was the purpose. But as teens, we began to investigate it. As we grappled with life's challenges, we wanted to find out where we were going. We had to take a risk and climb the Tree of Life to find out what fruit was growing there. But as life goes on, we discover that truth lies in the eating of the fruit. We do not know where we are going until we have arrived, until we have ingested its fruit. Then we have knowledge.

Here is a favorite story of mine. I again invite my sisters to identify with the male protagonist as if it were a female character. The characters of all fairy tales simply show the many components of our complex psyches.

Once upon a time, there was a fine queen who had a big old tree growing underneath her window. Every day she looked out and tried to imagine what kind of tree it was. So one day she sent out a proclamation to one and all, promising a reward to anyone who could climb her tree and bring back some of the fruit, but all the princes who tried fell out of the tree and broke their necks.

There was a young lad named Janos, the son of a swineherd, and when news of the queen's proclamation reached him, he felt a strong desire to try his luck.

He came to the queen's door and knocked, for in those days kings and queens lived among their people.

"I've come to see about the fruit of the tree underneath your window," he said, "as you asked in your proclamation."

"I hope you know what you are doing. Many have tried and failed already."

"Yes, ma'am," answered Janos. "I would just like to ask for a few things first. Let me have fifty nails, and a little hatchet and a wooden stool, and food to last me a week."

The queen was a little skeptical, but she agreed to Janos's request.

Janos started out at the crescent moon and climbed for a long time. When he got tired, he hammered three of his nails into the trunk and hung his little stool on them so that he could rest awhile. He ate a modest meal and slept on the little stool. Presently he came to a place where the trunk forked into three branches. One branch led to the east, the other to the west, and the third to the north.

He decided to go east, from where the sun rises. And there before him he saw the fruit of the tree, golden, ripe pears, ready to eat. Janos picked some for himself and ate them with gusto. Then, remembering the queen's request, he took out his little hatchet and cut a whole branch and let it fall. Down below, it began to rain pears. They covered the entire courtyard. People could wade in them, there were so many pears coming down.

But Janos continued climbing the eastern branch. Presently he saw before him a castle supported on a rooster's leg. It kept turning, always facing him, no matter which direction he chose. This confused our young man. He had fulfilled the queen's request, but curiosity was driving him now.

"Castle, stop turning," he called out. "It is I, Janos, who tells you so!"

But the castle just kept on turning. Janos pulled out his little hatchet and flung it at the castle, and this time it stopped.

In the middle of the castle, what should he see but a golden cradle dangling from a golden chain, and in it a beautiful sleeping girl!

"Ho, my beauty, wake up! It's afternoon already!"

The girl opened her sky-blue eyes. "Hello, Janos!" she said, as if she knew him. Well, that made him blink, and she smiled. "When you lay in your mother's womb, no larger than a poppy seed, I already knew we would talk together one day. . . ."

Janos was astonished. Clearly this was no ordinary girl, but a fairy woman, for how else could she know such things? In truth, Janos was encountering the Fate goddess, who knows all, and to whom past and future are all the same.

"We must hurry," she added, "because they are cutting down the tree."

This was dreadful. How could they cut down the Tree of Life after all the nice fruit it had given them?

Time was speeding now for our boy; his entire support system had been taken away. He could never go back down the way he'd come up. His childhood, parents, his entire village were all gone. He stepped into magical time.

"I would gladly go," he complained, "but I cannot walk in the air!"

"Don't worry," answered the girl. "I will let a thread out from my heels. You just step on it and you'll be coming safely along."

Here it is, the thread of life, spun out by the Fate goddess!

To walk on the thread required more then just a leap of faith from Janos. It required total suspension of his common sense, total surrender to his fate. Walk in the air. Sure. Do the impossible. Trust me!

But the fairy girl just shook herself and started out on her flight, leaving behind the thread for Janos to step on. Traveling in this way, they both soon arrived in fairyland.

This might be considered Janos's second destiny. A new alliance. A new cast of characters for his life. Totally new rules.

In fairyland, Janos and the girl entered a beautiful castle. When they were rested, the fairy girl said, "Listen, Janos, you are a clever young man. I want to hire you as my driver. You will drive my carriage every Saturday night when I go to the ball. I have a fine mare, whose four legs have been nailed to stakes, because she likes to kick a lot. You will take care of the mare, make her pull the carriage properly. As for the rest, we will see."

Now Janos had a job! *A new mission!*

Well, he went into the stable immediately to meet the mare. She was standing there shackled. Janos carefully liberated the four hoofs from their chains and tossed the stakes out to the compost pile. The horse spoke to him immediately.

"Eh, my good little master, it is wonderful to be able to move again as I please. I would like to ask you for a big favor now—give me a bucketful of rye to eat, for I am very hungry."

Janos got the rye and gave it to the horse. Then the horse asked for two buckets full of water, which she drank up.

"Eh, little master, because you have been good to me, I will do some good for you. Reach to the roots of my tail, and there you will find a little key. Under the threshold there is a chest; use the key to open it up. You will find in the chest three suits: one made of bronze, the second one of silver, and the third one of diamonds. Take those with you. Then just let things happen. You'll see—all will turn out all right."

Janos did as the magic horse advised, and waited for Saturday.

When Saturday arrived, the fairy girl got all dressed up for the ball. Janos drove the horse for two hours until they came to a beautiful castle, so bright with the many lights that burned within that it hurt his eyes to look at it. The fairy girl descended from the carriage and disappeared inside.

When they were alone, the horse spoke to Janos.

"Eh, little master, put on this bronze suit, and go and mingle with the guests at the ball. Don't stay longer than a half an hour. Just show yourself, but then hurry back to me. Then change back into your working clothes and wait for my mistress."

Janos followed his horse's advice.

He went into the ballroom and danced with a few girls, including the fairy girl. She did not recognize him in the bronze suit, but she thought he was very handsome. Soon, though, he excused himself and said that he had to go.

"Wait, let me give you a token so that you will remember me!" cried the fairy girl, and she gave him a beautiful ring. Janos took it and left the ball in time, changed back into his working clothes, and pretended to be asleep when the fairy girl came out of the castle.

"Hello, Janos! Have you seen a bronze prince come by?" she asked.

"A bronze prince? That would be a sight indeed," he said, "but I have seen nothing other than myself out here."

When he returned the mare to the stable, she asked him if everything had gone well. When he answered that it had, the horse told him that the next week he must take the silver suit.

Another week went by. On the next Saturday, once more they drove to the shining castle, and when the fairy girl had gone inside, the horse advised Janos to put on his silver suit and go inside, too.

For half an hour Janos mingled and danced. This time the fairy girl was even more taken with him, and gave him a golden ring. Then he left the hall, changed back into his working clothes, and when she came out, he pretended to have been asleep all the time.

"Have you seen a silver-suited knight coming out from the castle?" she asked, but he only answered as before.

Back at the stable, the mare asked him how it had gone, and advised him to take the diamond suit when they went the following week.

On the third Saturday, everything happened as it had before. When the fairy girl went into the ball, Janos dressed up in his diamond suit. Then he went into the ball and looked so dashing, nobody could resist his charms. The fairy girl totally lost her head, and this time the ring she gave him had a diamond. She ran after him when he left, but he managed to change clothes before she could catch him.

"Eh, little master," said the horse when they had reached the stable. "Tonight the fairy will ask you over for dinner. When you drink the wine, drop the rings into her cup so she will finally recognize you."

And so it went. The fairy girl offered wine to Janos, and when she looked away, he slipped the first ring into her cup. The fairy girl drank and when she had finished the cup, there was the ring.

"This is my own ring! How did it get here?" she asked.

"We'll see," answered Janos, pouring the next cup, and as he did so, he dropped the second ring into it.

"This is my golden ring! How did it get here?" she cried.

"We'll see," said Janos, pouring more wine, and when she finished it, there was the diamond ring in her cup.

Now the fairy girl demanded that he bring her the man to whom she had given those rings. Janos went into the stable and put on first the bronze, then the silver, and then the diamond suit so that she could recognize him.

The fairy girl embraced him finally and said, "You are the heart of my heart. I am yours and you are mine. Only death can part us!"

And they became man and wife and lived together in the castle and were happy. Hungarian fairy tales move fast and don't pause for much explanation about symbolism. It's understood that you already know the symbolic language. She had to recognize the three phases of the soul's journey (youthful is bronze; mature is silver; and divine is diamond). Even a fairy needs to grow.

But the story doesn't end here. This is only the second destiny for Janos. Now comes the third destiny.

"My dearest husband!" the fairy wife (for that's what she was now) said to Janos one day. "I have some business to take care of and must go away for a while. While I am gone, I want you to be in charge of the twelve rooms of our castle. Each day you should open the windows to air out the rooms, except the twelfth room—you should not open that under any circumstances. Here are the keys."

As soon as the fairy wife left Janos alone, he started opening the rooms up one by one. What could be in the twelfth room? he wondered. He had to know! He felt strong enough to face anything, so when he got to the twelfth room, he opened that up, too.

The key turned in the lock. Inside was a twelve-headed giant nailed to the wall by three nails.

The giant's twelve mouths opened. He said, "Hey, hey, Janos, thank you for opening the door. Nobody has been here to visit me for a very long time. Could you please, please, give me a glass of water?"

Janos was a good sort. He took pity on the giant and went to get him a glass of water. The giant drank it down, and as he did, out popped one of the nails off the wall.

"Janos, I implore you on your mother's soul, please bring me another glass of water!" the giant said.

"Sure," said Janos, and got him another glass.

The giant drank it, and as he did, out popped another nail off the wall.

"Dearest man, please bring me one more glass of water. I implore you on your own soul!"

"All right," said Janos, and gave the giant the last glass of water. As he drank it, the last nail popped off the wall and he was free!

The fairy wife had just returned. Before she could say a word, the giant picked her up off the ground and they disappeared as if neither of them had ever existed!

Janos was dazed. He had only meant to do a kindness, and now he had lost everything! But from the stable came a whinnying. It was his friend the mare, who knew everything that went on.

"Don't you worry," said the mare. "We'll try our luck again. Your wife has been taken to the Whispering River, seven countries from here. The giant brought her there to do the dishes."

Janos was flabbergasted. "Doing dishes? But she is a fairy!"

"Get on my back and we'll go and find her."

Janos mounted his mare and off they rode. For days and weeks, they went on. Sometimes Janos didn't even know where they were, but eventually they heard the whispering of the river, where the fairy wife was doing dishes in the cold water.

"Love of my life!" Janos addressed his wife. "Get up behind me on the mare—I have come to rescue you."

And so the fairy wife mounted the mare and they started back home. But the giant had a horse that had seven legs, and he could step over an entire country in one step. This horse knew what was going on and made a big noise with his pounding hoofs so that the giant could hear it.

"What is the matter?" the giant asked. "Don't you have enough to eat and drink? Don't you have a lovely fairy mistress?"

"I have enough to eat and drink, but master, the fairy mistress is gone! But don't worry, we have plenty of time to catch them. Eat and drink and take your midday nap," said the horse.

And so it happened. The giant slept his midday sleep, then mounted his horse, and they caught up with Janos in no time. There the giant plucked the fairy wife from behind Janos, threw her over his own saddle, and went back home with her.

"Let it be, little master," the mare said to Janos. "I see that we have to be more subtle. The giant's horse has seven legs, and I have only four."

The next day they went back to the Whispering River, where the fairy wife was again doing dishes in the cold water.

"Love of my life, listen to me," Janos said. "We cannot rescue you until you have found out where the giant keeps his power."

"I will try to find out," she said.

Then they heard the ground shaking as the giant approached, and Janos and his mare hid in the thick forest.

"Hey, new husband," said the fairy woman. "I cannot sleep for wondering, where do you keep your power?"

"And why should you want to know that?"

"I need to know so that I can honor it!" she answered him.

"Well, if you have to know, my power lies in that broom over there!" lied the giant.

The fairy woman picked up the broom and began to decorate it with ribbons and flowers.

"What are you doing now?" the giant asked.

"I am celebrating your power, husband," said the fairy woman. "I am decorating the broom because I don't ever want to leave you."

Now the giant started to trust her.

"Your other husband had no chance against me," he said, sitting down on the riverbank. "Only one horse in the world could have outrun mine. It lives across the seven seas with an old woman. If someone were to serve her for three days, which count as three years in our time, she would give him the horse in payment. But that will never happen, so you are safe with me."

But Janos was listening, and when the giant finally left for his dinner, he came out to say good-bye to his wife.

"Eh, little master," said his horse, "you had better take me back home because I cannot follow you over the seven seas. But I will give you some advice. Get a pair of boots made of one ton of iron and a walking stick made of half a ton of iron. Take those with you and try your luck."

The power that had helped Janos in his second destiny could advise him but not accompany him. Now he had to defeat a much greater, deadlier power on his own. First he got a pair of iron boots and an iron stick to take with him on the long journey.

He walked for a long time. When he was tired, he sat down in the shade of a beautiful tree to have a little food. As he started eating his bread and onions, he saw a little mouse nipping bites out of his bread. Instead of driving the little mouse away, he said to him:

"I have enough to share with you, mousie. Don't worry, eat as much as you like."

"Janos, you are a good-hearted man. Thank you. But because one good deed deserves another, take a few hairs from my back. You never know when you might need to call on me. If you take out the fur, I shall appear to you no matter where you may be."

"Thank you!" Janos said, and put the fur into his pocket.

He walked farther and farther, and presently he found himself on a little path that led straight up to an apple tree. But half of the tree was dead—only part of it was green and healthy.

"Apple tree, apple tree," he addressed it, "what has happened to you?"

"I am starving," answered the apple tree, "because a thief buried a chest of treasure beneath my roots, and now I cannot get enough food and water. But if you dig it up, little master, I will turn into a green tree again."

"I can do that!" said Janos, and started digging. And there beneath the roots of the apple tree he found the hidden treasure of gold and silver coins, which he took for himself.

"Thank you so much!" said the apple tree. "Now come and break a little branch from my green trunk, and when you take it out, I'll be there with you and help you."

Janos put away the little branch and went on his way.

His iron boots had worn way down, and his iron walking stick likewise, when he reached a big lake where two soldiers were shooting at a poor wild goose. The helpless goose was ducking under the water to avoid the bullets, but she was growing too tired to continue much longer.

"What are you doing?" Janos asked the soldiers.

"We are trying to shoot that goose, but she keeps getting away."

"What is she worth to you?"

"Three pieces of silver," they answered, "for that is what we would need to buy a meal."

"Here, take five coins," said Janos. "Drink to my health with the extra, and let the wild goose live."

"Thank you for saving my life!" said the wild goose when they had gone. "Now pluck out one of my feathers, and take it out if you ever need me."

"Thanks!" said Janos, and continued on his journey. When he had walked for three days and three nights more, he arrived at the holy well in which the waters of life flowed. Next to the well there was a wolf, who was dead and being eaten by maggots. Janos took his cup and filled it with water and poured it all over the dead wolf, and in a moment the wolf became alive again, as frisky as a puppy.

"Thank you for giving me back my life!" he howled. "Now come closer and pull out a hair from my back. You may need it in the future."

Janos added the hair to the rest of his magical treasures and continued on his journey.

At long last he reached the ocean. On the beach he saw a little snake, half dead. He stroked it and gave it something to eat. The little snake coiled itself three times and lifted its head.

"Thank you, kind brother!" it said. "I have nothing to give you, but I know you are going to see the old woman. When you enter to have a talk with her, leave the door a little ajar, and I shall come to help you."

Janos accepted the snake's offer and went on his way.

Presently he came to the roaring wild ocean. How was he going to cross? For a time he almost despaired, but then he remembered the apple tree and took out the branch it had given him. As soon as he looked at it, the entire apple tree appeared in front of him.

"What is the matter?" asked the tree.

"I must cross this great ocean, and I have neither boat nor ship."

"You were right to call on me," said the apple tree, and in an instant it grew into a beautiful ship.

As soon as Janos stepped on board, the sails shook themselves down and the ship began to move. They sailed and they sailed, until they came to the never-never land where the old woman lived. When the ship touched shore, Janos got out and climbed up to the house and knocked on the door. The door swung open, and he saw the old woman herself, sitting at her hearth.

"Good evening, dear old mother!" said Janos politely.

"You are lucky that you called me your old mother, otherwise I would have stuffed you alive into my rotten tooth. But tell me, what are you doing here?"

"I came in search of employment, and to try my luck."

"You came at the right time," said the old woman. "My servant just quit. I have three mares. Every day you must take one of them to the forest and bring back firewood for the hearth. The first day, take my gray mare, the second day my red mare, and the third day, take my black mare. Three days count as three years here. If you serve me well, I will reward you, but if you fail me, you get your head chopped off."

"I understand," said Janos.

After supper he slept the deep sleep of the tired traveler. The next morning he got up and went straight to the stables. He took out the gray mare and started for the forest. When they arrived, he put the horse out to graze while he stacked the cart with lots of firewood. At noon he was ready to return, but the horse was gone. He looked everywhere but couldn't find the mare!

To go home without the horse was certain death. As he was weeping with frustration, he remembered the little mouse, so he pulled out the fine fur and suddenly the mouse was right there with him.

"What's the matter?" asked the mouse.

"I have lost the mare that pulled that cart full of wood, and the old woman is going to chop my head off."

"You didn't lose the mare. She has gone down under the earth to a party, where a special gypsy band is playing for her. But don't worry, I'll go after her and bite the mare until she wants to come home."

The little mouse went down and found the mare, and he bit her ears until she had to return to the surface in order to get rid of him. When she did, Janos slipped the reins over her head and soon they were on their way home with the wood.

The old woman was not happy. "You have betrayed me!" she said to the horse. "You obeyed him and didn't hide away as I told you. You love this Janos, don't you?"

"No, no, I hid away, but to no avail. He drove me back out again."

On the second day, Janos went out gathering wood once more. And sure enough, the red horse also disappeared. Janos took out the hairs of the wolf, and in an instant, the wolf was before him.

"What is the matter?"

"Not only do I have to work hard to gather all this wood, but my red horse has disappeared."

"No it hasn't. Do you see the glass mountain? Upon its slopes a herd of sheep are grazing. The one that has a limp is your red horse."

Janos went and found the limping sheep, and when he put the bridle on its head, it became the red mare, and he hitched her up and they took the wood home.

This time the old woman was really furious. She beat the red mare, screaming that she had obeyed Janos because she loved him, no matter how much the mare protested that she had tried to hide.

On the third day, Janos took out the black mare, and the same thing happened: When it was time to go home, he discovered that the mare had disappeared. And so Janos took out his last charm, the wild-goose feathers.

"What is the matter?" the goose asked, appearing before him.

"The old woman's black mare has disappeared."

"No, she is only hiding behind the sun," said the goose. "I'll fly up there and beat at her with my wings until she runs back to earth once more."

And soon enough Janos saw the black mare coming, and before she could catch her breath, he had the bridle on her and was driving her home. And so the third day of Janos's service was done.

The old woman was very upset, but she had one more trick up her sleeve.

"Come, Janos, you have served me well. Let us drink some wine together to celebrate!"

Janos followed her down to the cellar, but he remembered how she had beaten the mares and he left the door ajar, calling for spirit help, and in another moment the little snake slipped through the door and began to whisper:

"The wine she will give you is a sleeping potion. You must pretend to drink it, but really pour it down your shirt."

The old woman was surprised when Janos stayed awake, but as he had completed her tasks, she concluded he must be a better magician than she.

"Very well, Janos, you have fulfilled your part of the bargain. What do you want for payment?"

"I want a little time to think about it," he replied.

When he went to his room, he left the door ajar so the little snake could follow him.

"Janos, don't accept anything she offers you," the snake said, "but ask for the little wooden eight-legged horse that is lying on the rubbish heap. When you get it, give it food and drink, and it will turn into a splendid stallion."

"Did you decide what you want as your payment?" the old woman wanted to know when he came out again.

"Oh, yes. I have enjoyed serving you so much that all I want is that little wooden eight-legged horse that lies on the rubbish heap."

"You don't want that! Why, it's all broken!" she protested.

"I want nothing else," Janos insisted, and finally the old woman gave in.

He carried the wooden horse down to the shore and gave it food and water as the snake had instructed him. In a moment it turned into a fine stallion, the fastest horse in the world. When he mounted, it flew fast like a thought back to the Whispering River, where his fairy wife was still doing dishes in the cold water. When she saw him, she was so very happy, her laughter rang out like a chime of silver bells. She jumped up behind him on the stallion and they headed for home.

The giant's horse heard all this and warned the giant.

"Janos has carried off the fairy woman on the stallion from the old woman who lives across the seven seas. You must run after him if you can, for I can't catch him."

But all the giant ever saw of the stallion was the dust he raised as he flew over the plain.

So Janos and his fairy wife went home to their castle, and there they stayed. And if they were not the happiest couple fairyland ever knew, then no one has ever said anything about it to me!

THE THREE DESTINIES OF HUMANKIND

They say that when the world was young we lived longer and had at least three lives. Our three destinies, ruled by Urdh, Verdandi, and Skuld, flowed eventfully one into another, a situation reflected in the continuing episodes of the old fairy tales. Later, when wars and kings made life sadder, the fairy tales changed, too, until they told only of the first destiny, in which the hero marries the princess and they live happily ever after—which was about until they were in their thirties. Most people didn't live long back then. Even at the beginning of this century, life spans were much shorter.

Now that we are climbing out of the Age of Pisces, with all its endless conflicts and wars, perhaps we will live longer again. Already people are noticing that they have more than one destiny. Like Janos, we find that the first quest leads to a new life, and just when we think that one is eternal, it changes as well. Many of us will make it into our eighties. This old story is becoming relevant once more.

Who is this story about? All of us.

In Hungarian fairy tales we don't have to worry about sexism. In Hungarian the pronouns "he," "she," and "it" don't exist. It is an ancient language where everything is referred to by the same word in the third person, "o," unless indicated by name. Sometimes a girl is the hero, sometimes a boy.

In this story, the females are the goddesses of fate: the queen, the fairy wife, and the old woman. Humanity here is represented by the boy hero. The pears that grow on the magical tree are the breasts of the Goddess—to eat them foretells a sexual initiation, and sure enough, he then finds the fairy girl. The fairy girl sleeps, her destiny not yet activated, and yet she already knows the shaman boy. They are fated to be together.

The girl tells him that his old support system is gone, they are cutting down the original tree, they have to move to fairyland. He has to trust her and "walk on air." Isn't this always the case when one is in love? But their relationship is not equal. The boy is clearly lower in status compared to the spiritual creature and has to work his way up to her level. The magic horse is the key to upward mobility—in fact, from that point on, many horses play a major role in the tale. (Horses are a constant in almost all Hungarian fairy tales. We were nomads until a thousand or so years ago. Our ancestors were quite close to their animals, especially the horse; it was the nomads' strength. Magically, the horse means transformation because it can carry you between worlds.)

The speaking horse who gives the three different suits to Janos is his first shamanic helper. The three suits are the three ages of destiny, the three incarnations of his evolving status. He wins the love of the fairy girl but then loses her because he lets the bad giant off the wall. The bad giant is in the twelfth room, the house of death. He lets Death out, and Death takes the fairy girl. She is in the grip of the big ogre, her ancient enemy, Death. Washing dishes in cold water refers to a mourning custom in the countryside. When somebody died, all the things left behind had to be washed in cold running water to purify them for further use by the living, which is the job of the wife of Death.

Tricking the giant by dressing up the broom is her symbol of will and purification. During the burning times (from the eleventh to the seventeenth century, women were persecuted as witches and burned at the stake) women often disguised their wands as brooms, a household item. A glorified broom is empowerment. The most powerful horse, which Janos must win to rescue his fairy wife, belongs to the old woman, who is, of course, the destiny goddess Skuld.

That she has an eight-legged wooden horse that can become alive and outrun Death's horse, who is only seven-legged, is interesting. Eight is the number of seasonal changes in a year, the spokes of the Sabbaths. It is the full circle around the sun. Janos has to earn his right to live through his third destiny, which he does by making alliances with all kinds of other magical beings, specifically the animals and birds he saves. A human destiny can only be completed if one learns to serve others. Janos not only serves the old woman by gathering wood (memories), but he helps the animals who work with him to outwit death.

Our little shaman is good-hearted; he loves all beings, and even saves a decaying wolf. The only mistake he makes is to help the giant, and even that pays off in the end, because it makes him grow. His good deeds bring success, and his love for his wife triumphs over death. The snake, who represents the cycle of rebirth, gives especially interesting advice to Janos, but in order to hear it, our hero must leave the door ajar—even the best advice is helpful only if you have an open mind with which to receive it.

This is more than just a fairy tale, it is a model for how to live and how to interact with other sentient beings and fulfill one's destiny. For women it is a story of identification with all things magical, requiring understanding of both the male and female principles of the universe. It is an exercise in claiming both humanity and divinity to give meaning to our lives. Women are not separate from men, from animals, from magical trees, from fairies, from anything alive. Women *are* humanity, and are embodied by all the characters in the tale. This requires us to move beyond separatism, not by regressing but by transcending it. By reclaiming all three destinies, we learn our true strength as individuals and as manifestations of the Divine Feminine.

Chapter Nine

Divination

How do you
know about
my fortune?
Do you think
my Dearest Goddess
would come
and give
my secret
away
so easily?

LATVIAN WOMEN'S FOLK POEM
NO. 54815.241

Divination was given to us by the Fates to keep us from losing hope. They have given us the tools such as the runes as a pool of wisdom and direct advice to help us navigate through life. Because you can use it throughout your life, this special sacred technology can give you guidance whenever you need it. I learned as a child to depend on divination for vision, and to show me a way out of difficulties. When times were hard, as they often were, my mother would take out her gypsy deck and lay out a horseshoe formation with them. Humming to herself, she would examine the cards for a while. Then her eyes would light up, because she had found the silver lining in the cloud. It didn't matter that she had lost her job or that we had nothing to eat for days. It was not important that we had to pretend to relatives that we needed a change to explain why we were moving in with them for a while. The silver lining was there—all she had to do was to follow the advice indicated by the cards.

I remember once when things were very bad after the war, the cards gave her the idea to put out a children's comic book, which we sold on street corners. My mother made up stories about me and drew all the pictures. Later in my life there was a time when I depended on divination for my bread and butter, when I was reading tarot cards for all kinds of folks, for hippies, stockbrokers, and winos on Venice Beach. I charged the stockbrokers a percentage if they made money from my advice, and read for the winos for free to accumulate good karma.

But my best story about divination comes from my mother's life. Although you can read for yourself, someone else can often see things for you more clearly, so my mother had her cards read once a month by her own reader, Magda. After one of these readings she came out of the room ashen white.

"Mom, what's wrong?" I asked.

"Magda found cancer in my right breast. I must see a doctor."

She went to see her doctor and, indeed, although it was still so small it was almost undetectable, the beginning of a cancer was there in her breast, just as Magda had said it was. With such early warning, the doctors were able to prevent the cancer from spreading.

As you can imagine, we were loudly and frequently grateful. After that, Magda always got the best Christmas presents from my mother, who said that Magda and divination had saved her life.

DIALOGUING WITH THE FATES

In the last quarter of the twentieth century we have seen a terrific rebirth of interest in our inner lives. This interest has manifested itself in myriad ways—through millions of books, workshops, festivals, and dream work, to levitation, channeling, crystals, and, of course, the use of tarot, the *I Ching,* and the runes to get in touch with the Fates. This wealth of sources provides us with a smorgasbord of spirituality. In typical American fashion, we mix and match, taking practices from all over the world and combining them to suit our tastes.

One of the fastest-growing megabusinesses in this country is selling goods and services via 900 numbers. If you look in the back of many mainstream magazines, such as *Cosmopolitan* or *Better Homes and Gardens,* you will find them. From looking at those ads, I think I know who their target audience is—women seeking to get in touch with their souls. This year I have acquired a 900 line myself (1-900-737-4637) because I missed the contact with the public that I had when I did tarot readings at my store. These days I am a full-time writer and spend most of my time at my computer, or walking with my dog, who is a good companion but doesn't talk much. Why are psychic hot lines so attractive to many women? They are like the old custom of visiting the temple, consulting the Sibyl, the wise woman.

Women are more likely to acknowledge the mystical side of their soul. While there is no sexual discrimination in the psyche—both sexes are equally affected by the magnetic fields of the earth and the stars—most men in our present culture don't like to admit it. In the West, divination, like many spiritual practices, is mostly a woman's passion.

Back home in Budapest, once a week the women washed their hair, then went to find out about the next week by consulting the cards. In Hungary, fortune-telling is a cottage industry and always has been. It usually takes place in the intimate setting of a home, where a small group of women gathers in the kitchen with comfortable chairs, a nice tablecloth, and a piping hot teakettle on the stove. The psychic is most often a woman of some maturity. You don't want a young one, as her range is limited. For this work a saucy, experienced woman is best, one who has been around the block once or twice. She comes in, you share some tea, then she unfurls her hand-embroidered flowery cloth and rolls her deck of cards out of its silk sheath. Looking into your eyes, she begins to "read."

All cultures have developed methods by which to question the Fates, to gain a glimpse into the future. I think that reading for the spirit is a most important human skill. This ritual of sharing information about our soul's nature requires that we learn how to use some method of divination well. I don't think it matters much which one.

A friend of mine from old Yugoslavia reads tea leaves. I have no clue how. But she feels she is getting messages for the spirit from the forms taken by the little tea pieces that are poured out onto the white cloth after the tea has been consumed. Like a Rorschach inkblot, the shapes of the tea leaves suggest meanings. My mother could read palms, others read feet. The features, the skull, the teeth—all have been used successfully by cultures around the world for divination.

I myself have quite a history with divination. I first learned to read gypsy cards from my mom but was not very good at it. Not until I encountered the tarot did I hit my stride. There are only thirty-two cards in the gypsy deck—not much variety compared with the seventy-eight images of the tarot. With the gypsy deck I couldn't figure out how the transitions were made from utter sadness to joy.

Once I learned something about the philosophy of the Tree of Life, my understanding of the tarot expanded into wonderful concepts that went beyond fortune-telling, and I began to comprehend the stages that the soul must go through in order to successfully rotate through the circle of life.

I loved the tarot. During my hard times in the middle of my first Saturn return, no matter how much my heart was hurting, I could read the tarot and end up with hope. The cards taught me that life was not a terrible thing. Even death served a noble function. Nothing was ever wasted. No pain was unnecessary. The cards told me that we are all travelers in motion. Nobody can really say what's going to happen; they can only give us a clue here and there so that we can be better prepared for what the Fates have in store for us.

When I opened my candle shop in Los Angeles, fortune-telling was illegal, although the law was not always enforced. I ended up playing a major part in changing that law. I've told this story in my earlier book, *Grandmother of Time* (HarperCollins, 1989).

As soon as we had opened the doors of my store, The Feminist Wicca, women started asking for readings. It was an amazing feeling, casting the tarot patterns and realizing that these accidental

combinations actually spoke to the women deeply, and my inter-
pretations made sense whether I understood them or not. Eventually, lines of women waiting for readings started to form in front of
my little candle shop. The police noticed our sudden popularity and
sent a policewoman to obtain a reading from me. I had no idea it
was against the law.

But I should have known something was wrong. When the
policewoman came into my reading room, suddenly there was an
intense smell of cat shit in the store. We had no cats, so I was puzzled as to where the smell could be coming from, especially since it
smelled fresh. I looked everywhere and finally found the pile underneath my reading chair! Cat shit to me smells trouble. I told the
woman she would have to reschedule—I couldn't work under
those conditions—but she helped me to clean it up and begged me
to read for her. She said she couldn't get away from work again.

I still remember her cards. Her significator was the devil. I
asked her, "Do you work in places where you feel tied down, or
where there are other people who have been restricted?" She went
pale, because that's as close as you can get to a description of the
police department via tarot. In fact, everything I told her was true,
and she left quite impressed.

However, that didn't matter to the two plainclothes policemen
who came in after her and arrested me for fortune-telling. I was
taken to jail and had to be bailed out to go home. There was a lot of
publicity in Los Angeles. The witch trial took four days, with a jury
filled with Chinese women who didn't know a thing about European paganism. When "witch" was translated into their own language, the term meant "worker of evil magic." They made up their
minds that I was guilty.

It was painful to be on trial for divination. Nobody knew much
about the Goddess in 1975; in fact, this trial was the vehicle that put
women's spirituality on the feminist map. Women decided that if Z
is threatening the patriarchy this much, she must be doing something

right. So I became known as a visionary spirituality activist for the first time.

We lost the case but won the issue. I appealed for nine years—quite a long time to fight for the dignity of women counseling one another via divination. By the time I won, I no longer read cards. I was a full-time writer. It took nine years and another case from Long Beach (against a woman who was a palmist) and, of course, getting the Honorable Rose Bird on the California Supreme Court to strike down this law. When this case came before her, she struck down all laws against divination and laughed the case out of court. Now the sidewalks of Venice teem with tarot readers, and a whole revolution has happened in the area of psychic awareness.

From this desire to learn what's going to happen, to learn how we can conduct ourselves better to achieve our dreams and avoid the pitfalls before us, come the incredible, rich systems of divination practiced all over the world. Underlying the predictive aspect, however, is a philosophy that teaches that ultimately we are not alone. We are not forgotten, abandoned, worthless. Just the opposite. There is meaning in each existence, meaning that comes from its accumulated whole. It tells us that the universe, our home, is intelligent, complex, and fair. We are given what we need. We are expected to do our best and discover our gifts. The Fates expect us to use our shortcomings as well as our assets. All that is given has meaning.

DREAMING

When we sleep, our souls go back and visit in the realm of the shadows, the realm of dreams, the realm of the Fates. In dreams we can get instructions.

Emese, the mother of Hungary, did—she dreamed up our entire country and its fate thousands of years ago. Emese was the First Lady of the nomad Hungarians, and she wanted to conceive a child, but for a long time she couldn't. Then one night she saw in a dream Father Attila (yes, Attila the Hun, who in Hungary has a rather different positive reputation than elsewhere) riding toward her down the Milky Way with his men. Atop the staff of his banner perched a great turul (an ancient huge hawk), the albatross of the steppes. As she watched, the bird suddenly took flight, all the way into Emese's tent. It settled into her lap, where it rested its head and went to sleep. Then Emese saw a river starting up from her body, and it branched out and became many rivers that encircled the entire earth.

The dream filled her with joy. When she reported it to the local *taltos,* the shaman Torda, he interpreted it as a prophecy of greatness. Emese would conceive a child, a boy, Torda said, who would lead the Hungarians to a land that would forever be their own. The nomad peoples were running out of room to roam in. It was time for the Hungarians to settle down.

In due time, Emese bore a boy-child, who was named Almos (Dreamy) because he was first seen in a dream. Torda directed us to march to the borders of the old Hun country. The *taltos* was received kindly by the peaceful king who lived there. The young shaman asked for a handful of dirt, a cup of water from the river, and a handful of grass as tribute. The king saw no threat in this. He ordered his men to give the *taltos* what he asked for. They even gave him a white stallion. And so the *taltos* returned to the Hungarians with the symbols of their country—the water, the earth, the grass, the animal.

The descendants of Emese then celebrated a great ritual and made many prayers to her, putting all the offerings on the altar. The next morning, before the good king and his people even woke up, the Hungarians descended the slopes of the mountains and flooded into the country below. They didn't kill the people, for there was enough room for them to live side by side, but they took possession of the country. When the kind king asked why they had done this, the shaman answered, "You are not our enemy, but you have willingly given away your country to us. These lands that were once the domain of our father, Attila, are now again ours as Emese saw in her dream."

Can you imagine claiming an entire country based on a dream? What would the real estate business come to? But this story lies at the heart of Hungarian history. Our very origins are based on magic and dreams. Sometimes it seems as if we depend on omens and signs from nature more than on the events of the real world. After all, magic and fate-full dreams have worked for us just fine.

Significant dreams can turn a life around. Native Americans sought dreams to find the totem animals for their spiritual journeying. In dreams, animals can visit you and give you advice, clarify things if you are plagued with doubts, strengthen your instinctual self. We are all players in the dream world.

For a long time, Western civilization didn't appreciate dreaming. "Oh, you are only a dreamer!" they cried, as if that were a sin. It was only recently that sleep researchers discovered that without sleep, in which dreams come, we can die, and now psychiatrists analyze dreams for symbolic content that will help them understand their patients and their problems.

In dreams, the unconscious speaks to us, or perhaps it is the soul. But folk tradition knew that all the time. Dreaming has always been a direct line to converse with the divine.

In Hungary we have all-night vigils in blooming apple orchards on the days and nights dedicated to the Boldogasszony, the Virgin of Hungary. Women spend the night praying in the orchards. Others party, eat, and celebrate, then sleep on their embroidered healing blankets on the ground.

WORKINGS: DREAM DIVINATION

Dreaming is a kind of divination that anyone can do. To call in prophetic dreams, tie a blue (the favorite color of the goddess of the night) silk scarf loosely around your left hand and sleep with it. As you tie the scarf, say clearly, "Tomorrow morning I am going to remember and write down my dreams."

Don't go to bed too late. The dawn hours are when the most prophetic dreams occur, and you should be well rested by then. Eat lightly the night before, and don't take any drugs, not even a little wine. Near your bed, place a bowl of clear water (which should be replaced every day) and some cut flowers. These are resting places for the fairies that bring good dreams. Dream catchers, wall hangings made with natural objects, dried flowers, silk paintings, etc., on your wall will brighten up your bedroom and assist you in catching good dreams.

Keep a dream journal handy by your bed, and when you wake, even before you open your eyes, go over in your mind what you've been dreaming about. Then write it down before doing anything else—dream memory vanishes within five minutes, so you have to catch it in time.

OMENS AND ORACLES

The wise women and men of ancient days sought omens in nature. Some of that lore remains in the forms of superstitions, such as the belief that a black cat crossing the street is unlucky. You have to watch out, though—many omens are considered evil now because they are survivals of old pagan belief. Cats, for instance, were sacred to a number of ancient goddesses, such as Freyja in Scandinavia (later considered a goddess of witches) and Bast. Cats were worshiped in Egypt because people saw the goddess Bast in their demanding sexuality and excellent mothering of the kittens that resulted. Because cats protected the storage houses of grain from vermin, it's possible that when the black cat crosses your path, she may be telling you, for example, to protect your "houses of grain."

When you need an omen of what Fate has in store, you can still seek prophecy in nature. Go outdoors. In the wilderness the powers of the spirit are stronger and communication is easier, but a yard or a city park can work as well.

The first step is to articulate the question you have. Let's say you have a problem, such as whether to change jobs. Frame your question so that it can be answered yes or no. Now look around you and think of a natural event that is possible in this setting—for instance, it's no good saying that if a fish leaps up it means yes unless you are near water! Make an agreement with the powers of nature that is simple and clear, such as "If some birds fly toward me from the west, it will mean yes, but if they come from other directions, the answer is no."

Then sit down and wait. Suddenly you will see something that fulfills your criteria and answers your question—birds fly, a wind comes up, you hear the birds' song. Some friends of mine have tested this by asking several times to see if they get the same answer. That's missing the point—once should be enough, and besides, answers rarely change even if you change the rules. If you are too skeptical, the spirits will get annoyed and you may get no answer at all.

In the ancient world, oracles were located at sacred places where the earth energies were particularly strong, such as a cave, the source of a river, or a grove where there were legends of the appearance of spirits. The famous sites of the classical world, such as Cumae and Delphi, had temples and a priesthood to maintain the site and support the oracle, but every district had its sacred spot. Often these rural oracles were "staffed" by the nearby country-women, who took turns in the dark, standing in for the Goddess, listening and responding to the petitioners. The woman who received the answers felt the petitioners' burdens lightened, trusting in the providence of divine presence who had spoken to her through her sister. This form of oracle work was still practiced in China in the 1950s. We call it channeling today.

In Scandinavia, oracles were given primarily by women, called Volvas or *spβkonas* (speaking women), who traveled from place to place accompanied by a group of younger women they were training. When they stopped at a farmstead, they would take a little time to make contact with the spirits of the place, and then perform the *seidh* ritual, attended by everyone in the neighborhood. The young women sang the sacred song to call the spirits, then the *spβkona* went into trance and answered everyone's questions.

Diana L. Paxson has recovered this practice and now teaches it in workshops all over the country. With her group, Hrafnar, she performs oracular *seidh* at various festivals, much as the Volva and her group moved from place to place in ancient times.

PERSONAL DIVINATION

One way to take charge of your own destiny is to learn a divination system that you can use at home for yourself. My favorite, obviously, is the tarot. There are many, many decks available, all of them featuring the same basic cards, but each with its own slant and style. It's great fun to get to know one. These days, every metaphysical-book store carries a few of them. Tarot decks are also available from catalogs.

Your first step is to buy a deck of tarot cards. Contemplate the images without reading up on them at first, and just see what kind of feeling you get from them. Once you've made their acquaintance, you may want to pick up some books discussing interpretation.

Then memorize one card a week, by pulling one at random. Let's say you have cleared your mind and pulled the Temperance card. Now for the rest of the week you can think about what that concept means in your own life. The Temperance card usually shows an angel balancing on earth and water, holding two golden goblets from which she seems to be pouring water back and forth.

Temperance is about balancing the good and bad, balancing the outflow and intake of energy. You learn that this image is an angel, who encourages you to work for others, to have an altruistic goal. You learn in living that if you pour out energy for the good of all, you are automatically taken care of by the universe—it will come back to you. This is a wisdom borne out of practice. With each card, you increase your spiritual vocabulary of images. By the time you have absorbed all seventy-eight images, you will be happier and more secure than before, because your psyche will have been transformed. Wisdom does that to one's life; it creates inner peace. And inner peace is mental health.

You can use a similar procedure to learn the runes, the original magical writing, another deep source of wisdom. I recommend them as strongly as the tarot. As images, the runes are more abstract than tarot cards, but they are easy to draw, and once you have learned them, you can make yourself a set on slips of paper whenever you have a need for them. Many stores now sell rune sets, or you can make your own by painting the runes on small stones.

When you are familiar with the meanings of the runes, you can draw them at random from a bag and lay them out in a tarot spread or in the three Norns pattern—three in a row for the past, three for the present, and three for the future. Pay attention to the way they affect one another as well as their individual meanings. You can also draw a rune in the morning to tell you what is going to happen that day. For instance, if your rune for the day is Sowilo, the Sun, because the sun travels from east to west, it might indicate that you may be doing some traveling. Or it might mean that you are on the right track and that whatever you are engaged in will bring victory. Of course, it also might mean, simply, that it's going to be a sunny day!

Our information on the meaning of the runes comes first from the Old Norse and Anglo-Saxon rune poems, and second from contemporary rune masters such as Edred Thorsson, Kveldulf Gundarsson, and Freya Aswynn. For an accurate and spiritually inspiring view of the runes, their books are recommended.

A remarkably easy way to get your angel to communicate with you is by using a pendulum. I had a friend who went grocery shopping with her crystal pendant and held it over each food she was considering, asking if she should eat it or not (the agreement was that the pendant would swing in a circle if the answer was yes). The pendant advised her what to eat and she lost a lot of weight (sixty-five pounds) following the spirit diet.

Teardrop-shaped pendulums are sold for divination purposes, but you can use almost any reasonably heavy pendant on a chain. Hold the chain loosely about four inches up from the pendant. Sit comfortably and hold the pendulum out in front of you. Ask it how it will indicate yes, then try to hold your hand steady and wait. The pendulum may move erratically for a few moments, but eventually it will steady. It helps if you think strongly about something for which the answer is definitely yes while you are doing this. Then repeat the procedure, asking how it will indicate a "no." Once you have calibrated your pendulum, you can start asking your questions. Your angel inside will move the pendulum in answer.

Dowsing rods can also be used in this way. You can make your own by cutting up two coat hangers so that you have two L-shaped rods, the shorter ends being a little longer than your fist. Hold them loosely in your fists and calibrate as you would for a pendulum. You can also use dowsing rods to find things you have lost in your house.

Prophecy is a healing folk art and it is coming back. All these divination systems say the same thing: Life is manageable. Life is difficult but good. You are born, grow, suffer setbacks, and retreat. You focus within, then ripen, bring your fruits to harvest, then sink down again, become compost, and are reborn. Each moment of our lives is like a drop of the ocean that can be analyzed to show the content of the whole sea. In the moment lives infinity.

RITUAL: WORKING THE WIND

One of the most important symbols of fate is the living wind. You can use this ritual in preparation for your divination work or simply to feel the power of the Fates.

My mother prayed on the north wind. She said the north wind, Nemere, brings the great souls into the world, so she always honored the Fates on the north winds. The eastern winds bring in revolutions and new ideas and artistic inspiration. The southerly winds bring in trade, new cultural influences. The south winds are sexuality. When they blow, it is a good time to have sex and to make great babies. The south wind brings a desire for reincarnation. It brings peace and sometimes hurricanes. When the west winds blow, it's a good time to die. The west wind collects the souls after life is done and takes them behind the north wind, where they wait until they are blown back again.

"The winds of change," "the changing of the winds," "gone with the wind," "blowing in the wind"—all are well-known expressions to indicate powers beyond our realm. These are part of the divine force. Nobody owns or controls the winds. The winds touch us all equally. They are impartial and they operate at random, and they carry our messages swiftly.

My mother prayed on the four winds when we needed help. It didn't matter if it was sickness or an enemy, trouble of any kind was well within the winds' powers to divert. She opened the living room window and stood there whispering on the air until a little movement was felt.

> *Now you come, my mother's ancestors,*
> *with the north wind, I summon you here.*
> *You listen to me call,*
> *you respond to my voice.*
> *On the north wind I summon you now*

with my praying breath.
Now you come, my father's ancestors,
on the east wind, I summon you here.
You run with the red tempests,
stir up the gray dust.
You hear my voice calling,
upon my praying breath.
Now you come, my dearest animal ancestors,
I call upon you on the south winds.
Bird-formed spirit, shaman woman,
I welcome you here with my praying breath.
Now I call on all the departed,
the west wind's wings will bring you here.
You make the moon rise,
gently ruffle the seven seas,
be here in your breath,
be here and listen to me. . . .

A little breeze was the "ancestors' breath," she said. She waited until she felt this evidence that the winds were listening, then she would explain her trouble, in regular words, as if talking to her own mother.

But the wind was better; this greater mother was the north wind. It was the north wind that was the most magical, the most unpredictable, the most fateful. If you could tell your troubles to the north wind, you were as good as saved. Your problem would be positively resolved. The north wind loved helping people when prayed to.

The four winds are the breath of the earth. The winds fly everywhere, touch everyone. All creatures must breathe the same air. All must exchange breath, a symbol for the spirit, for the soul. At death we "expire"—let out our dying spirit with the last breath. The winds contain the breath of all those who have passed on and all those who are alive today. The same air circulates throughout the earth.

Part of the song called "Breaths," from the CD *Sweet Honey in the Rock,* goes:

> *'Tis the ancestors' breath*
> *When the fire's voice is heard,*
> *'Tis the ancestors' breath*
> *In the voice of the waters.*

When you pray on the winds, take some fine sage, sandalwood, cedar, or frankincense and myrrh. Go to a mountaintop or any kind of open space where the air circulates and you can feel the wind. Unless you are standing on bare rock or concrete, you should contain your incense or smudge stick in a censer that will keep sparks from flying. Light the incense, and when it is going well, turn around three times so that the smoke whirls around you. Say:

> *I summon the winds to witness my prayers,*
> *I summon the winds to carry my prayers!*
> *Carry my prayers to the four directions,*
> *to the four directions, in the skirts of the Fates.*
> *In the skirts of the Fates*
> *blow deep to the center of the soul.*
> *To the center of the soul, the center of my life*
> *blow kind winds, blow warm,*
> *bring me love and delight,*
> *bring me healing and light.*

Sit down and meditate on your life. Are you content? Count your blessings and thank the Fates. Tranquillity is a blessing; so is being overwhelmed by trivia. There is even a goddess of trivia—her sacred scrolls are the shopping lists and laundry receipts. Destiny unfolds in its own time—it is hard to see what is happening while we're in the midst of it. As a fish doesn't know it is in water, we don't usually know where the winds of change are taking us until we're there.

Feel those winds whirling around you as your incense burns. Talk to them . . . thank them . . . ask them to help you:

> *Breath of the gods, mighty winds,*
> *you who touch all equally,*
> *come to me, for I need your counsel.*
> *Come to me from the four directions:*
> *come, great spirit carriers from the north,*
> *come, great idea gatherers from the east,*
> *come, feelings of love and pleasure from the south,*
> *and come from the west, where the souls find eternal rest.*
> *My breath welcomes you, hear my story. . . .*

Whatever you have to say, whisper it to the wind. Don't worry about what people will think of you—you're not talking to yourself, you're talking to the wind. In many traditional cultures, worshiping the wind is an accepted way for the individual to communicate with the divine. If there was no wind when you began your ritual, after you have made your prayer you will begin to feel a little breeze. When that wind stirs your hair, you know the Fates are listening.

CHAPTER TEN

THE BIG WEB

"This is the Age of Aquarius, the Age of Aquarius, the Age of Aquari-uuuhs!"

I remember sitting in a coffeehouse in Greenwich Village back in the sixties, listening to that chorus. The musical *Hair* had brought hippie culture to the stage, and you could hear its most famous song everywhere. Suddenly astrology was in, and the first thing you got asked at a party was, "Hey, man, what's your sign?" Back in the sixties, Astrology was Destiny.

It has taken me many years to begin to understand how our own fates are interconnected with the larger fate of our world.

The Fates work on many levels. Each living thing has its own life span, some long and some (to our thinking) very brief indeed. In terms of the life span of the earth, though, human lives are no more than a blink of the eye. But the Fates spin their threads for all things, and they measure out the ages of the earth as well as our own.

Today there are only a few sciences that pay serious attention to the interconnections among energy, matter, and meaning that produce destiny. Of these, astrology, which many do not accept as a science, has contributed the most. It occupies an odd position in our intellectual universe, discounted by the intellectuals but avidly followed by the masses. Zodiac columns are the most consistently read parts of the daily newspapers. Whether we believe or not, we all know our sun signs.

Whether or not astrology tells us anything about the stars, it tells us something very important about ourselves. Humans have found significance in the movements of the planets since the magi of the Middle East first studied them, and the fact that now we are sending machines to photograph them makes no difference. We will never lose interest in the stars. Why should we, when they are the only ones who say to us, "Hey, you are unique in the universe! You have special stars and special paths. You count! You are part of us!"

Astrology is a map of energies, spinning destiny on the wheels of the planets themselves. Never before has the image of the great weavers of fate made more sense to me! Look at the pattern they are weaving, in and out of the ages, sub-ages, and conjunctions with one another. The planets not only influence our daily lives but determine the characteristics of generations, give us a kick in the butt when needed, incite us to revolutions. In the motions of the planets, the Fates weave history. After all, we are made of those stars ourselves. It makes sense to examine those heavenly bodies as our own blood/star relatives.

The Greek Moirae, the three Norns, the three Fates, have their own three stars between the constellations of Gemini and Taurus. They look like three stars in the form of a delta; their symbol is the triple triangle. If the Saturn return cycle is the major pattern in human life, what is the equivalent in the life cycle of the earth?

An equinox is the point in the year when the poles of the earth have rotated to a position in relation to the sun where the days and nights are of equal length. Although within a solar year the earth's position in relation to the constellations—the sun signs—changes so that they move forward, the position of the earth's axis in relation to the stars at the spring equinox moves in a very gradual circle in the other direction so that the sign against which the vernal equinox rises changes over very long periods of time—the ages of the Earth.

When the Babylonians calculated the zodiac, the constellation of Aries rose in the east at the time of the vernal equinox. Around the time of the birth of Christ, the earth had shifted enough so that the rising constellation was Pisces. As we approach the twenty-first century, the heavens are shifting so that the constellation of Aquarius is rising nearer to the equinox. This movement will take a while to complete. Not until the twenty-fourth century will Aquarius rise due east at the spring equinox, which begins the astrological year. In the meantime, there are sub-ages within the age, and we are in a sub-age of Aquarius right now.

THE GREAT YEAR

It takes around 25,800 years for the vernal equinox to precess through all twelve signs of the zodiac. This we call the great year. The great years don't begin on cue, they come in gradually, like a slow dawn, then gain strength. Nor are they the same length. Some great years take longer than others.

If you slice up this 26,000-year period into twelve zodiac signs, you get the ages of the earth, about two or three thousand years apiece. Some constellations take longer than others to roll by. But looking at the great years helps us to understand how the Fates guide the destiny of our world. Considering that planet Earth is 4.6 billion years old, she has had 177,000 great years already. It was an endless beginning. Each great year had twelve ages—you might say she has been around the bend a few times.

In addition to this, we imagine each age having twelve sub-ages, so that in a 2,150-year period the earth moves through the entire wheel of the zodiac. Each sub-age will take about 179 years. These sub-ages display the influence of the zodiac signs within each of the ages, adding atmosphere and focus to the big picture. Let us look at the big picture first. Imagine the three kind Old Ladies at their task, turning the wheels of time ever so slowly but surely. How do the events of our earthly history match up with the zodiac ages? This is the first web.

The Age of Virgo: 12,722–10,573 B.C.

Historians begin their work with the origins of writing in the Age of Aries. I prefer to look at archaeology as well and to take it back at least to the Age of Virgo. This was a long, long period, most of it coinciding with what archaeologists call the Paleolithic, or Old Stone Age. From this age comes the first human art, and evidence of spirituality and culture. Cro-Magnon humans lived in caves in the cliffs. In the deep caves, the womb of the Goddess, they painted the walls with magical images of all the animals they hoped she would send to the hunters. But in the caves where they lived, beside those first hearths, they placed statuettes of the Goddess herself, the first images of divinity in human form.

Ancient Europe was filled with small Goddess statues— "Venuses" were everywhere. The people prayed to female deities, created underground temples, and directed their worship to the Creatrix Matrix. But a new culture was coming. In the Paleolithic, the men hunted and the women gathered mostly vegetable foods. Like people in hunter-gatherer societies today, they undoubtedly realized that certain kinds of plants grew in the same places every year. Toward the end of that age, someone (probably a woman) got the idea of deliberately scattering some of the seeds they collected on the ground, and agriculture was born. At the same time, some animals were beginning to be domesticated. The goddess who had watched over the Paleolithic hearths presided over the first experiments in agriculture. Virgo is the Lady of the Harvest, medicine, beauty, women, and sciences. In those times, agriculture and domestic sciences were developed, the first written records were kept.

The Age of Leo: Circa 10,572–8,424 B.C.

The Age of Leo saw the beginnings of the Neolithic—the New Stone Age. The first villages began to appear at the end of this period. Agriculture and trade became established. Just as the influence of the Virgin of the Harvest extended into the following age, in Leo, the Goddess became the Lady of the Lions, enthroned with her hands on the lions' heads or, later, riding in a cart which they pull. This image appears from the Middle East to Scandinavia, arguing for an extremely early diffusion. Lions still decorate palaces and kingly places, portraying nobility.

The Age of Cancer: Circa 8,423–6,275 B.C.

This is the period during which Neolithic culture flourished. Appropriate to a period whose sign is one of water, humans discovered the usefulness of traveling by boat during this time. Communities were built on the shores of lakes, by rivers, and near the sea.

In a more protected environment, more children were able to survive. It is probably at this time that the women who tilled the fields and gardens began to understand the influence of the moon on both agriculture and their own bodies. With a food surplus available for the first time, men were able to go farther afield. Coastal and deep-sea navigation made trade possible, and obsidian, flint, marble, and shells were carried all over the Mediterranean.

The Age of Gemini: Circa 6,274–4,125 B.C.

The next age saw the flowering of Neolithic culture. With trade came communication; new ideas were springing up everywhere. By this time a variety of food crops were being cultivated, and all the standard farm animals except for the horse had been domesticated. Villages began to grow into towns, especially in the Near East and the Fertile Crescent.

Religion in the Neolithic Age continued to have a female focus, but now the single Goddess became a pair as she was joined by, in turn, sons and lovers. Art reflected the idea of the female: circles for completion, spirals for the cycles of life, crescents for the moon, and animals—the bull, the ram, and the pig—for the sources of life. Bird and water imagery decorated the images of the Goddess. Simple shrines developed gradually into temples.

As new ideas proliferated, people discovered how to work copper and gold. Both weapons and ornaments evolved swiftly, and the first symbol systems, precursors of writing, appeared. In the Fertile Crescent, India, and Egypt, tribal cultures were developing into civilizations, but as yet, societies were relatively egalitarian and peaceful. It was during this time that the great rituals that mark the agricultural year evolved in Europe to become the basis of a religious system that survives in folk culture to this day.

Toward the end of this period, however, the first major challenge to this emerging civilization appeared. New peoples appeared from the steppes, nomads traveling in horse-drawn carts and chariots. To withstand or incorporate these new tribes, the settled cultures were forced to change.

The Age of Taurus: 4,125–1,977 B.C.

With Taurus—powerful, stubborn, settled—recorded history begins. Taurus represents possessions, edifices, earthly wealth. Wendy Ashley, a mythic astrologer, says that the constellation of Taurus stands for the maiden aspect of the Goddess. It is a fate archetype, along with the constellation Virgo, which stands for the harvest, and the constellation Capricorn, which stands for the crone when the earth lies fallow. So the fate triangle is Taurus, Virgo, Capricorn.

Although Taurus is a bull, in most breeds of cattle the female is horned as well. The image of the horns stands for a Venus-dominated age, when the V of the horns can represent the female genitalia, the curve of the fallopian tubes, the essence of fertility. In Egypt, Hathor, goddess of love and fertility, was crowned with cow horns. Nuit, the divine mother, was represented sometimes as a woman and sometimes as a great cow.

In masculine form, the winged bull with the head of a man appears to guard the gates of Mesopotamian palaces. In a Greek sculpture, the Fates themselves, as the Charities or the three Graces, are shown in between the horns of the sacred bull, lover of the Goddess. In Taurus, all the achievements of the previous age were grounded, supported, integrated as a permanent part of human life.

During this period the civilization of Egypt was established in a form whose basic characteristics were to remain unchanged for four thousand years. The civilizations of the Indus Valley and the Fertile Crescent took shape, and though new peoples moved in and names and languages and dynasties changed, the cultural continuity was clear. In Northern Europe, the megalithic cultures were building monuments of stone that still inspire awe today.

The cultures of the south needed this strength. In order to withstand the incursions of the horse people, they had to fortify their cities by developing armies and war leaders. The evolving hymns and myths of Inanna, patron goddess of Sumer, show not only how she acquired all the blessings of civilization for her people, but tell of the developing tension in her relationship with her lover-consort, Dumuzi the shepherd. When she undergoes her transformation in the underworld, Dumuzi establishes himself as supreme lord in her palace.

In the myth, Inanna emerges from her ordeal strengthened and takes back her palace, while Dumuzi is condemned to spend half the year in the underworld, but the threat to female rule has been made. In the Age of Taurus, although the feminine principle was still acknowledged as the source of sovereignty, and royalty might descend in the female line or the king might be consecrated by making the Great Marriage with the Goddess, whether patriarchal tribes conquered or the native peoples changed in order to fight them, more and more actual power passed into the hands of men.

In the Age of Aries, the retreat of the goddess religions was to continue.

The Age of Aries: 1,977 B.C.–172 A.D.

All things must pass, the ancient wisdom goes. The Age of the Ram, who batters his way to victory, could also be called the age of conquerors and assorted bullies. Humanity had begun with cultures in which the female principle of the universe was worshiped and emulated, the women were respected, and their labor of love—the creation of children—was not exploited. But as wave after wave of invaders moved south and westward, leaving their own earth goddesses behind and bringing with them their tribal gods, with them came the value of might over right.

The discovery of bronze gave men much better weapons, and the Iron Age that followed made them more effective still. Aries is the Age of the Warrior; the sacrificed ram of Abraham and the golden fleece of Jason show the way to conquest. The goddesses were still worshiped, but they had become the daughters, sisters, wives, and sometimes even the victims of the gods.

The Age of Aries encompasses most of what we know of ancient history. Great civilizations arose, with mighty temples and walled cities built by slave labor and defended by armies. Empires, from Sumer to that of Alexander the Great, rose and fell. Rome, which was to become a greater empire still, was founded and began to expand.

Our major cultural heritage from the Age of Aries is the Old Testament. All the values are there—an eye for an eye, a tooth for a tooth. The human family reflects the heavenly one, in which a mighty father rules, whether on Ararat or Olympus, descent is traced through the male line, and the rape of women or the annihilation of a people are justified if they serve the gods' purpose.

The Age of Pisces: A.D. 172–2,320

This sign is characterized by suffering and martyrdom, struggle and confusion, but also by great creativity and imagination, although our current age has downplayed those positive Piscean qualities. The two fishes heading in opposite directions are in constant conflict, a duality that cannot be resolved. Pisces is also a mystical sign, in which there is a strong motivation to seek spiritual knowledge.

Because Pisces is a mutable water sign, it is overly impression-able—the previous age, Aries, made too deep an impression and colored the entire, current age with Arian feelings and values. The New Testament puts its stamp on the psyche of these times. We never have really known the full positive Pisces spirit, because we have allowed the past to haunt us.

The great religions of this age, Christianity, Buddhism, and Islam, were founded by men who were seeking purity and spirit, but because they were persecuted by the people of their own times, the movements they founded were eventually co-opted by the cultures they had been intended to oppose. Christianity, for instance, inherited the bureaucratic structure and language of the empire that crucified its founder. Concepts of sin, guilt, and sacrifice became part of the worship of the new male gods. This symbolism of martyrdom justifies sacrificing not only men but women and children. It glorifies self-sacrifice, and eventually requires it—demands it—especially from women.

Pisces could have been an artistic age, characterized by mysticism and gentleness, oriented toward pleasure. And it is true that we have had some great artists live during this age, but few of them have been happy. Serving the collective consciousness carries a heavy price tag in loneliness, poverty, discrimination, and lack of appreciation in this age.

Only today and only in "show business" are artists rewarded at all—and maybe too much so, since their money isolates them and makes them a target for exploitation of various forms. We pay entertainers and then consume them like so much psychic junk food. In a true artistic age, we would support our artists and treat them like human beings; we would not be angry at them for being able to sing, dance, act, paint, write, or philosophize ("Yeah, why don't you get a real job like me!"). In the Age of Pisces, we both hate and love our celebrities. In the new age, we will appreciate them but not canonize them. Good psychic food will enable us to grow up emotionally and not need this ersatz life lived through the rich and famous.

The Age of Aquarius: A.D. 2320–4469

The Age of Aquarius is looming up over the horizon, and its influence is beginning to make things change. As the Information Age gathers strength, the mist is starting to clear.

Within each of these great ages of the Earth, the entire zodiac has been represented by "sub-ages" of approximately 179 years each. The first sub-age, lasting from A.D. 172–351, was Aries, intensifying the influence of the preceding Great Age for another century. The last sub-age of this period will be Pisces, providing a reprise of the last two thousand years. At the moment, however, we are in the sub-age of Aquarius (1962–2141), which is giving us a preview of the influences and themes that will dominate the next age.

What will it be like? It is interesting to note that both of the major television series about the future, *Star Trek* and *Babylon 5*, are set in the twenty-third and twenty-fourth centuries. *Star Trek* became a cultural icon at the beginning of the sub-age of Aquarius, in 1962. *Babylon 5* is the creation of a man who grew up in the early sixties.

The universe of *Star Trek* is more utopian than that of *Babylon 5*, but both feature societies in which racial tolerance and gender parity are accepted parts of the culture. In *Star Trek*, Earth hosts the headquarters of the United Federation of Planets, which seeks to promote harmony among all beings. In *Babylon 5,* Earth is currently going through a reactionary period, but the space station itself is attempting to lead an alliance of sentient beings into a new age.

The Sub-Age of Aquarius

In 1962 the sub-age of Aquarius began; it will continue for about the next 179 years. Within each sub-age, the turning of Pluto is the generational "wheel of history" in the hands of the Fates. They turn this wheel very slowly, keeping it in the same sign some ten to twenty years, in order to define the mood and energy and focus of a generation. If there is a true wheel of karma, distant Pluto, last to be discovered among the planets, is it.

Let's take a look at how Pluto has influenced the history of our times.

Which generation are you traveling with? According to astrologist Geraldine Hatch Hanon, in her book *Sacred Space,* the generations are as follows: Pluto in Cancer, 1914–1939; in Leo, 1939–1958; in Virgo, 1958–1972; in Libra, 1972–1984; in Scorpio, 1984–1995; and in Sagittarius, through 2008.

People who were born in Plutonian Leo were concerned with power, freedom, or the lack of either. Power to the people! we cried. Those years bred many dictators and warriors, but also their opposite, the flower children. In the early sixties (already Plutonian Virgo), the civil rights movement flowered as Martin Luther King Jr. found his mission in life. Suddenly cleaning up our social act was desirable. Justice seemed possible, freedom seemed possible, change seemed possible.

The baby boomers (born in Plutonian Leo) reached draft age just in time for the long, festering wound of the war in Vietnam. The generation that questioned power now had to deal with service, which is the message of Virgo. President Kennedy told us, "Ask not what your country can do for you, but what you can do for your country," and instituted the Peace Corps. President Johnson declared the War on Poverty, and new social, educational, and medical programs gave hope to many.

Serving the human race with war didn't make sense anymore; a paradigm shift had occurred, and the young people realized that their lives were on the line. They were willing to risk their lives to win civil rights for blacks, but not to impose capitalism on Southeast Asia. The generation gap became a political force.

Some fled to Canada, while others went to Vietnam and lost lives or limbs. Many of those who stayed home began to march to protest the war. Glorification of war belonged to the previous ages; in Virgo, peace and harmony, long-haired males, herbal tea, and equality and sensitivity ruled.

The same young people who marched against the war thronged to the concerts of the Beatles, and later to the Jefferson Airplane, the Band and other groups who sang the songs of the new era. The unleashed emotion of the girls who screamed for the Beatles was the first cry of the open female power that was to come.

The hippie movement reached its peak with the Summer of Love in 1967—"Tune in, turn on, drop out"—as Virgo influenced the emphasis on inner life for the first time for the masses.

The Beatles and the stars who followed them were role models for a softer, sexier, shaggier male, less threatening, less macho, more romantic. Men who loved women. Suddenly clothing was bright and flowing, and drugs and gurus encouraged people to explore their souls. Do your own thing!

The concert at Woodstock epitomized this time. Thousands of young people gathered together for a weekend of turning on with music and drugs and the contact high. We prided ourselves on being nonviolent, on sharing resources, on enduring hardships by helping one another. Woodstock was beautiful. We were feeling that having a big party like that proved once and for all that our philosophy of nonviolence was the way of the future. There were no fights among the men; everybody was gentle and good-natured and stoned on the finest grass and mushrooms. The musical arts and love bloomed. Wavy Gravy, one of the performers, cried out, bloodshot eyes flashing, "We must be in heaven, man!" And briefly we were—in Virgo heaven.

It was at about this time that the women who had been making the coffee while their boyfriends planned the demonstrations began to protest their roles. Women began to organize again, and the third wave of feminist political struggle in this century began.

The girls who had screamed at concerts now got on the Pill, another Virgo invention. Suddenly pleasure was available to both sexes without the fear of pregnancy. The flower children began to fade, and in the seventies, women as a group developed a consciousness of themselves as competent, equal partners in rebellion and peace. The women's liberation movement became very strong; now sisterhood was powerful.

Suddenly, women were applying a "Virgo-style" analysis to injustices they had never thought to examine before. They demonstrated for abortion rights, burned the symbols of their servitude—bras, false eyelashes, makeup, high heels. Radical women protested the Miss America pageant in Atlantic City, crowning a sheep as queen.

One of the things that got reexamined during this time was religion, as women suddenly realized that they didn't have to worship a male god. Goddess figures appeared in hippie art, and here and there, groups of women began to explore their own spirituality. On December 21, 1971, I called together a group of women in Los Angeles to hold a seasonal celebration for the first time with the Goddess as the spiritual focus. We were aided by the last rays of the powerful Plutonian Virgo in our effort to rebirth the Goddess traditions. Women connected with one another as souls and assumed responsibility for their spiritual lives. For the first time since the fourth century, women stood up as priestesses of the Goddess and praised her by at least ten thousand names.

As Pluto moves through the zodiac, some epochs are shorter than others. The energy of Plutonian Libra is directed toward justice and law, relationships and communications. Arts, music, and health have also been affected, but most of all, Libra made connections. This generation desired balance.

In Plutonian Libra sweeping changes were brought in in the way people related to one another privately and collectively. It exposed that which was not equal and made it intolerable. Never before had the sexes discussed their relationships so deeply. Men realized that they needed to learn how to please a woman—a novel idea. The ideal of marriage became one of equal partnership; the time for sexual equality had come. Couples lived together without being married, or married after they had tried living together for a while.

Divorce rates were rising, because women were no longer willing to put up with abusive relationships, and as they made progress in the business world, they no longer needed men to support them. California first instituted "no fault" divorces in 1969. Women discovered they were multiorgasmic. Workshops for preorgasmic women cured those who still couldn't find their clitoris. Just a year into this vibration, in 1973, women got back their right to abortion! No more forced motherhood or bloody, botched abortions.

But perhaps the major change was in the woman's position in the working world. A good example is Iris Rivera in Chicago, who in 1977 was the first woman who refused to make coffee for her boss, arguing that it wasn't in her job description as a legal secretary. She was fired but her fate radicalized the other secretaries. Working women led public actions against the petty ways in which they were made to feel inferior. They conducted workshops for bosses in how to make coffee, and they even got Rivera's job back!

Pluto brings out into the open that which is hidden or denied. The Watergate scandal revealed the president's misdeeds, and in 1974 he was forced to resign. Plutonian Libra energy kicked him out, because he was out of balance, had abused his power. Other political changes were coming. In 1984, Geraldine Ferraro was the Democratic candidate for vice president. Increasing numbers of women ran for office; from that time on, women have marched steadily toward equality in all fields.

These days, the "old girls' network" is in place. Women network, establish professional ties. Libra taught us cooperation; we learned to help one another, find female mentors. Even the dress code at work is getting more relaxed, though we still want to look smart. Complaining is out, power lunches are in. This phase ended with hope and direction for women, and the belief that if we work hard, we will get ahead.

In 1984, Pluto entered Scorpio, remaining there until 1995. To start things off, Sally Ride became the first American woman to take a ride in space. Women broke the "glass ceiling" and moved into senior executive roles. Now Pluto was in its own home sign and became correspondingly powerful. And don't forget that this web is influenced more and more by the deepening of the sub-age of Aquarius, the framework in which all this is taking place.

Scorpio energy is very sexual, brooding, hidden. Life and death and rebirth are its themes, but it also shows us hidden potentials, hidden truths. It likes to stir up hidden sins, hidden hurts; it likes to create discoveries. The threat of AIDS and the new understanding of how it spreads is very Plutonian. The whole human race is interconnected sexually, and regardless of sexual orientation, the virus can reach us all, a danger that has transformed sexual relationships for both gay and straight couples. The free-wheeling sexual smorgasbord of the seventies is a thing of the past. Monogamy is back! Protected sex is back. Love has never gone away.

With this Plutonian change has come a resurgence of all kinds of spirituality, from fundamentalist Christianity to neopaganism, Goddess spirituality, and the New Age. New religious movements have grown astonishingly quickly, partly because of technological advances in communications (sub-age Aquarian influx!), especially computers, and the emergence of cyberspace. Electronic consciousness is transforming the world faster than ever before. Everyone is jumping on the Internet; everyone wants to communicate everything, all the time. We have entered the Information Age. No longer just helpers, women gain high regard in business and leadership. Women have proven to be superior managers. In cyberspace there is no sexual discrimination. Aquarian technology suddenly leaps into the future; we don't even understand where it will all lead, but we can be sure women will be part of it.

Another kind of awareness that has grown is the understanding of the danger to our planet that comes from the thoughtless use of technology. Children and adults alike have become united in concern for the earth. Earth-oriented ecology groups have gained acceptance. Ordinary men and women fight for the planet along with movie stars and scientists. (Aquariuuuus!)

In the areas of sex, death, and rebirth, all that was hidden is being revealed—homosexuality, child abuse, incest are the main topics of the talk shows. Churches are being sued by aging altar boys who were molested by priests, and military men who abused underlings are being brought to trial. Tabloid television features the worst of humanity. Television news brings the crises from Bosnia and Africa into our homes. We can no longer plead ignorance of what humans have done to the planet and to one another.

In this period we also began to require higher moral standards from our leaders. We elected the second-youngest president in our history, and the first of the baby-boomer generation to hold that office. The female vote was a significant factor in both elections. Women finally started to vote together since we have won the vote.

Pluto in Scorpio has brought hope as well. In this period a men's movement rejecting the old images was born. *Iron John* by Robert Bly was a best-seller. Men now feel free to cry, to drum in tribal costumes in the woods, to lament over the loss of their fathers. The men's movement is not yet interested in reclaiming men's mysteries, but some spiritual men are working on it. Although an "angry white male" vote carried a mean conservative Republican majority into Congress in 1992, support for this angry male agenda is waning as the Scorpio phase ends. The O.J. Simpson trial was the last act. As we move into the next Plutonian era, people are losing interest in freaks, in meanness, in revenge, and in hurting women.

Pluto entered Sagittarius in 1995. The image of the zodiac for this sign is a half-horse, half-man, with a drawn bow and an arrow aiming high. This half-and-half figure is Chiron, the wounded healer, who combines animal sexuality and spiritual wisdom. The energies of Sagittarius favor brand-new values, rituals, public revels, common sense with drugs, hearty good times, and positive sexuality, but also the search for higher consciousness and connection with our instinctual nature.

A brand-new set of values is coming into force: pleasure with common sense, physical activity, youthful energy, foresight, high goal orientation. Real progress will be made in space travel for the first time since the sixties. New Age inventions will come on the market. Sagittarius loves freedom, philosophers, and the whole spectrum of religions; it fosters education and understanding between nations. Sagittarius brings higher consciousness; energized by Pluto, this may result in a fundamental and long-lasting shift in consciousness.

This is the fateful step that will kick us into the twenty-first century. Sagittarius's soaring arrow points us into the future. In a just cause, his anger will strike with full righteous power.

This historical phase has begun with the reelection of Bill Clinton in 1996, with the help of a strong female vote. He represents the new male—an attractive, youngish man who is smart, survived abuse, sophisticated, sexual; who is compassionate and knows how to bend, give and take, be slick. Americans like people who are slick, in spite of the complaints against it. We like a president who is flexible, who favors education and advancing our civilization. In fact, Bill Clinton is perfect for the Sagittarius energy. (It also helps that he chose a strong, competent woman as his wife, the queenly, compassionate Hillary.)

Remember the seventies and all that friendliness and loving behavior? It will come back, but with caution. Sagittarius loves to party with friends. This Plutonian era will be hopeful and profoundly spiritual. Except for a few people who are trapped in millenarian anxiety, people will project happy things for the twenty-first century. Because of this high optimism, we may see another surge in births, a second boomer generation. Space exploration will be supported; medical discoveries will be made (conquering the virus at last); achievements will flourish. Sagittarius likes the healing arts, and many cures that have been kept under wraps will be released to the public. Significant progress in treating AIDS has already been announced. I predict the cure will be found in this era, as well as the cure for cancer. Our species will conquer the invisible viruses, our true enemies. There will be many other breakthroughs as well, as people are inspired by the new millennium.

Women will continue questing for higher goals. The Aquarian TV star Oprah daily tends to the souls of the collective females on the couch. We will have ambition in all areas; a pride in being human beings will be a major motivator. Humanitarian activities will increase. The politics of mean-hearted anger is going to disappear. Complaining will be out, while hard work, inspiration, and high goals will be in.

Television will drop the ugly tabloid freak shows and concentrate on shows with an element of spirituality. Fantasy, magical story lines, romance will be back. Women's spirituality will become important on a global scale. The Goddess will be visible to women and men alike. We will see bigger attendance for all goddess community gatherings. After the new millennium begins, fear and guilt-ridden religions will lose the young.

There will be more work on racial and sexual equality. Sagittarius likes justice and fair play. What dirt will be stirred up here by Pluto will have to do with religious lies and exploitation, greed, senseless violence, and abuses of authority. Moral standards will be high for our elected officials, who will not be allowed to cheat and lie and abuse and still hold office.

In 2008, Pluto will enter Capricorn. Capricorn represents the existing structures of our lives, and the way we live will undergo a major rearrangement. No more commuting downtown to work—home offices and home businesses will be the mode. Everything will be connected through the electronic media. People will have many ways in which to earn a living, but, as always, education will remain the currency for success.

The old work ethic will be back, but with a twist. Capricorn helps us to establish ourselves, and in this era, we will get to redefine ourselves in terms of the new millennium, and as a species settle down to some real maturing.

After Capricorn, Pluto goes into Pisces, at which point the times will reflect the positive aspects of the Piscean vibration, which we have seen little of thus far. Imagination will rule, escapism through virtual travel and dating. Pleasure, healing, and creativity of all kinds will be treasured.

Finally Pluto will arrive in Aquarius within the sub-age of Aquarius, giving us a true preview of what the Age of Aquarius will mean. The swift changes that the Aquarian double vibrations bring can be dangerous, but they can also quickly sweep the faulty past away like lint. Our heroes will be real people, with real lives, as we turn away from celebrity worship.

I wish I could stick around to see that—well, maybe I will come back! I would like to live in a time when human beings have learned to live together; when higher consciousness is our main focus; when all major humanitarian problems are being solved; and when more cures are being found. Aquarius is the ruler of health and service, medicine and technology. The arts will flourish, sexual discrimination and racism left behind. But we will have new problems caused by changing technology. There may even be new forms of humanity. And we will still have the task of healing the earth, which will take many generations to accomplish.

The universe unfolds as it should. The future improves as the Fates turn the wheels in our favor. Hard times of humanity are behind us—the dark ages, the awakenings, the terrible wars, illusions. We did learn a lot and are still learning.

Now is the time for humanity's flowering. This is the best time ever in our history to be alive, to be a conscious holy player on the wheels of time. Blessed be!

BIBLIOGRAPHY

Ashley, Wendy. *Goddess in the Sky* and *Astros-Mythos*. Self-published. P.O. Box 14, Peaks Island, Maine 04108.

Bauschatz, Paul. *The Well and the Tree: World and Time in Early Germanic Culture*. Boston, Mass.: University of Massachussetts Press, 1982.

Belanger, Sheila. "Homeward Bound: An Astrological Perspective on Women's Midlife Cycles," *The Beltane Papers Magazine,* vol. 10. Lammas, P.O. Box 29694, Bellingham, Wash. 98228-1694.

Benjamins, Eso, trans. *Dearest Goddess: Latvian Folk Poems.* Current Nine Publishing, 1985. Last known address: 5319 Manchester Drive, Suitland, Md. 20746-4407.

Caputi, Jane. *Gossips, Gorgons, Crones: The Fates of the Earth.* Santa Fe, N.Mex.: Bear and Company, 1993.

Conway, D. J. *Falcon Feather and Valkyrie Sword.* St. Paul, Minn.: Llewellyn Publications, 1995.

Cullen, Kathryn Dupont. *The Encyclopedia of Women's History in America.* New York: Facts on File, 1996.

Eliade, Mircea. *Shamanism: Archaic Techniques of Ecstasy.* Princeton, N.J.: Princeton University Press, 1964.

Eliot, T. S. *Complete Poems and Plays.* New York: Harcourt Brace, 1952.

Fox, Matthew. *Illuminations of Hildegard of Bingen.* Santa Fe, N.Mex.: Bear and Company, 1985.

George, Demetra. *Mysteries of the Dark Moon.* New York: HarperCollins, 1992.

Graves, Robert. *The Greek Myths,* vol. 2. New York: Penguin Books, 1960.

Greene, Liz. *The Astrology of Fate.* York Beach, Maine: Samuel Weiser, 1984.

Griffith, Elisabeth. *In Her Own Right: The Life of Elizabeth Cady Stanton.* New York: Oxford University Press, 1984.

Hanon, Geraldine Hatch. *Sacred Space.* Ithaca, N.Y.: Firebrand Books, 1990.

Harrison, Jane Ellen. *Themis.* Atlantic Highlands, N.J.: Humanities Press, 1977.

Kraditor, Aileen S. *The Ideas of the Women's Suffrage Movement.* New York: W. W. Norton, 1981.

Moore, Thomas. *Care of the Soul.* New York: HarperCollins, 1992.

Nelson, Richard K. *Make Prayers to the Raven: A Koyukon View of the Northern Forest.* Chicago: University of Chicago Press, 1983.

Nies, Judith. *Seven Women: Portraits from the American Radical Tradition.* New York: Viking Press, 1977.

Peary, Linda, and Ursula Smith. *Women Who Changed Things: Nine Lives That Made a Difference.* New York: Scribner, 1983.

Pennick, Nigel. *Runic Astrology.* Oxford: Capall Bann Publishing, 1995.

Plato. *The Republic.* Introduction by Desmond Lee. New York: Penguin, 1987.

Sagewoman magazine. P.O. Box 641, Point Arena, Calif. 95468-0641.

Sheehy, Gail. *New Passages.* New York: Random House, 1995.

Smith, J. *Epic Lives: 100 Black Women Who Made a Difference.* Detroit: Visible Ink Press, 1993.

Star, Gloria. *Optimum Child.* St. Paul, Minn.: Llewellyn Publications, 1988.

Stone, Merlin. *Ancient Mirrors of Womanhood.* Boston: Beacon Press, 1984.

Weir, Alison. *Women of Achievement: 35 Centuries of History.* New York: Harmony Books, 1981.

Wilshire, Donna. *Virgin Mother Crone.* Rochester, Vt.: Inner Traditions, 1994.

Zinn, Howard. *A People's History of the United States.* New York: Harper-Perennial, 1990.

Hungarian Sources

Bakay, Kornel Kik. *Vagyunk? Honnan Jottunk?* Tradorg Tikett kiadas, 1994.

Bede, Anna, and Kohalmi Katalin. *Sámándobok, szóljatok.* Budapest: Europa könyvkiadó, 1974.

Erdèlyi, Zsuzsanna. *Hegyet hàgèk, lötöt lèpek.* Budapest: Magvetö Könykiado, 1974.

Forrai, Sàndor. *Küskaràcsontòl Sulveszter estèig.* Budapest: Muzsák Közmüvelödesi kiado, 1975.

Jung, Karoly. *Az emlèkezett ùtjain.* Forum, 1993.

Kandra, Kabos. *Magyar Mythologia.* Hidfö Baràti Köre kiadàsa, 1978.

Krudy, Gyula. *Álmoskönyv.* Budapest: Magvetö Könyvkiadò, 1966.

Kulcsàr, Zsuzsanna. *Inkvizicio ès Boszorkány pörök.* Budapest: Gondolat, 1968.

Mora, Gyula Ferenc. *Hetvenhèt Magyar Nèpmese.* Budapest: Könyvkiado, 1986.

Nagy, Olga. *Hösök, csalòkàk, ördögök.* Cluj, Kriterion, 1974.

Pocs, Èva. *Szem meglàtott sziv megvert.* Budapest: Prometeusz Könyvek Helicon, 1986.

Ràdulyi, Jànos. *Villàm Palkò.* Ion Creanga könykiadó, 1989.

Ràth, Vègh. *Istvàn Varàzsvesszö.* Budapest: Gondolat Kiadó, 1979.

Timaffy, Dr. Làszlò. *Tàltosok, Tudósok, Boszorkànyok.* Györ, Hazànk, 1992.

Tomaffy, Laszlò. *Ràbaköz ès Hansàg.* Novadat, 1991.

About the Author

I was born on January 30, 1940, the feast day of Pax, Goddess of Peace, at a time when her worship was quite forgotten in Hungary. On that Tuesday, my father bought the local paper, which told him that the worst winter ever was pounding the country. The north wind was howling.

I grew up in dire poverty, spending my childhood in the ruins left by the war. The only time I had regular meals was when my parents gave me over to the nunnery in Pècel, where I was introduced to the rituals, processions, and incense dedicated to the Queen of Heaven and fell in love with the spiritual life and prayer, and with the Queen of Heaven. Although I knew from the time I was fourteen that I would be a writer, I didn't know then that I would help to bring back the worship of the Goddess on a global scale.

I attended the protests during the Hungarian revolution in 1956, but when the Russians came back and killed thousands of my fellow students, I decided to escape. I walked out of my country— literally. At eighteen I won a scholarship to the University of Vienna. At nineteen I emigrated to America, married my childhood boyfriend, and gave birth to my two sons, Làszlò and Gàbor.

As I left my Urdh years behind me and entered into the Verdandi phase of my thirties, I became another woman. I changed my name, moved from New York to California, and discovered a new mission through the women's liberation movement—to unleash the spiritual component within feminism and to bring back the women's mysteries, which empower all women. This work has consumed me—every breath I have taken and every word I have written has been to promote the Goddess. My path has been successful. I've published several books. *The Feminist Book of Lights and Shadows* was reissued as *The Holy Book of Women's Mysteries.* When I moved to the Bay Area, I published *Grandmother of Time* about the lost holy days of the Earth and its sister book, *Grandmother Moon,* about the lunar holy days. As the eighties unfolded, I wrote *Goddess in the Office* for the new woman in the workplace and *Goddess in the Bedroom* to honor sexuality and having fun. Now, in the very last of my Verdandi years, I have written here about the three Fates to show how all goddesses are these original old ones and how humanity has never really left behind the customs, prayers, and beliefs in Lady Luck and her sisters.

As I move into the third destiny of my life, ruled by Skuld, I already feel different. I find myself yearning to write about animals and my Hungarian heritage. Who knows where all this is going to lead me? I live life open-hearted, open-minded.

I have established a phone line to keep in touch with my readers and give spiritual advice, psychic readings, and mentoring to women who need direction: 1-900-737-4637. Every other year I design and organize the Goddess 2000 International Goddess Festival so that women can connect with each other and weave the web of the Fates. To be part of a living movement of spiritual rebirth, write to us and come to the festival:

Women's Spirituality Forum

P.O. Box 11363

Oakland, CA 94611

(510) 444-7724 (phone and fax)

My website is www.netwizards.net/ZBudapest

Blessed be!